THE HIGHBURY ENCYCLOPEDIA

Other titles in the same series:

The Anfield Encyclopedia by Stephen F. Kelly
The Elland Road Encyclopedia by Paul Harrison
The Old Trafford Encyclopedia by Stephen F. Kelly

THE HIGHBURY ENCYCLOPEDIA

An A-Z of Arsenal FC

Stephen F. Kelly

MAINSTREAM
PUBLISHING

For Judith, Nicholas and Emma

First published in Great Britain in 1994 by
MAINSTREAM PUBLISHING COMPANY (EDINBURGH) LTD
7 Albany Street
Edinburgh EH1 3UG

ISBN 1 85158 659 8

A catalogue record for this book is available from the British Library

Phototypeset in 11/13pt Janson by Intype, London
Printed in Great Britain by the Cromwell Press, Melksham, Wiltshire

ACKNOWLEDGMENTS

A particular word of appreciation should be given to Steve Hale, John Broughton and Cliff Butler, who have supplied most of the photographs in this book. Thanks should also be given to those at Mainstream Publishing who have been involved with this project, including Bill Campbell, Peter Frances, and Claire Simpson. I would also like to thank Steve Raw for the design of the jacket, Ian Wilson for his expert knowledge of the Gunners and my agent, John Pawsey, for his continuing encouragement. My gratitude, as ever, goes to my wife, Judith Jones, and children, Nicholas and Emma.

ABANDONED. A number of games involving Arsenal have had to be abandoned over the years. The usual reason was fog, particularly in the early years of the century when London was renowned for its pea-soupers. Only one game has ever been abandoned because of a waterlogged pitch – and that was in 1909, before the club moved to its present home. Only two games have been abandoned at Highbury since the war: the first, against Aston Villa in January 1954, as fog descended, and the second, in December 1967 against Sheffield Wednesday, as a snowstorm struck, reducing visibility to a few yards and causing players to slip dangerously on the pitch.

ADAMS, TONY. Essex-born Adams joined Arsenal as a schoolboy in November 1980 and made his debut in November 1983 against Sunderland at Highbury shortly before signing professional forms. Arsenal lost and Adams made only two more league appearances that season. Over the next couple of years Adams played only intermittently and it was not until George Graham took over as manager that he made his real breakthrough into the first team. But once the manager had shown confidence in him, Adams was to be a regular, making 62 appearances during the 1986–87

Tony Adams

season and 58 the following season. In February 1987 he also won his first England cap as England beat Spain 4–2 in Madrid. He has since gone on to collect many more caps, having already played at most levels for England, including youth and under-21. Now an established favourite at Highbury, he won a Littlewoods Cup winners medal in 1987 as Arsenal beat Liverpool 2–1 and then won league championship honours in 1989 and 1991. In 1993 he added an FA Cup winners medal to his growing collection and a second League Cup medal. A year later he won a European Cup Winners Cup medal. He was the PFA Young Player of the Year in 1987. During the 1987–88 season he replaced Kenny Sansom as team captain. Although he was sometimes criticised in his early years, Adams has grown in stature with each new season. He is now a tower of strength at Highbury, always committed and setting an example on the field. In the 1994 European Cup Winners Cup final he played a captain's role, holding the Arsenal defence against the quick-witted Parma attack. It had been one of his most memorable seasons with the club and one that ranked him among the finest post-war Arsenal defenders. Unfortunately, his private life has not always been as exemplary as his role on the field. But Adams is a player at his best when the going is tough. Without him Arsenal are only half a side.

ADDISON, COLIN. Signed from Nottingham Forest for £45,000 in September 1966, Colin Addison was expected to play a major part in the Arsenal side as Bertie Mee began his rebuilding programme. A scheming inside-forward, he never really fulfilled his promise and in September 1967 he was sold to Sheffield United for £40,000. He had played 31 games for the Gunners, scoring ten goals. His footballing career never really took off but at least he was to enjoy more success as a manager with Hereford, Newport, Derby County and Atletico Madrid.

AGGREGATE SCORE. Arsenal's highest aggregate score in Europe is the ten goals they scored against Standard Liege in the European Cup Winners Cup in 1993. Arsenal scored three goals at home and seven in the away leg in Belgium.

ALLISON, GEORGE. One of the greatest Arsenal managers, Allison had the unenviable task of having to take over from Herbert Chapman in 1934. Until then Allison had been a journalist. He was born in Stockton-on-Tees in October 1883, where he began a career in newspapers. But he was always fascinated by football and at the age of 21 became assistant secretary of Middlesbrough Football Club. By 1906 he had moved to London, where he resumed his career in journalism. For more than 35 years he was the London correspondent of the *New York Herald.* He soon became a fan of Arsenal and for many years reported on their games. He later became their official historian, edited the club programme and then in 1926 joined the board of directors. He became manager-director and when Chapman died he assumed responsibilities for team selection and was known as secretary-manager. Arsenal were at their height – they had just won a second successive championship – but Allison, much to his credit, kept the team at the top. They won their third successive title the following season and then another championship in 1938. They also won the FA Cup, beating Sheffield United in the 1935 final. The intervention of war, however, ruined Allison's plans. His record signing Bryn Jones had lost the best days of his playing career and Ted Drake was also absent by the time the war was over. Allison then faced the mammoth task of having to rebuild – a task that proved beyond him. He retired in May 1947 and died ten years later. Although Allison left much of the day-to-day running of the team to his assistants, there is no doubt that he had a fine eye for a player, signing Drake, Crayston, Copping and Jones during his years in charge. He was also something of an impresario, a brilliant public-relations man and someone who must be especially credited for helping to stamp Arsenal's name on the map of world football.

ALLISON, IAN. Signed by Terry Neill in October 1983 on a free transfer from Colchester United. He went on to play 75 games for the club, scoring 30 goals, making him good value. But, while Allison had his merits, he was hardly a diamond in the Arsenal side. His greatest moment was probably a goal against Spurs in the Littlewoods Cup semi-final but his greatest disappointment followed as he was left out of the side for the final. He later played with Stoke and Luton before making a sentimental return to Colchester.

AMATEURS. Perhaps the most famous amateur ever to play for Arsenal was Bernard Joy, who won ten amateur caps for his country between 1934 and 1937. He was also captain of Great Britain at the Berlin Olympics in 1936 and was the last amateur ever to be capped as a full England international, when he played against Belgium in the same year. Joy also won an FA Amateur Cup winners medal with the Casuals in 1936. Although Arsenal boasted many amateurs in the early days, only a few have played for the club since the Second World War. One of the most notable was Kevin O'Flanagan, who was a double international, representing Ireland at both football and rugby in the immediate years after the war. O'Flanagan was also a doctor and was unable to play in many Arsenal games, particularly the away matches, because of his medical commitments.

ANDERSON, TERRY. Anderson came through the Arsenal ranks, winning England youth honours, but he never quite matured into the player he had once promised to become. Nevertheless, he notched up 216 appearances, scoring seven goals, and was then sold by Billy Wright to Norwich for £15,000 in February 1965. He enjoyed better days with the Canaries, however, helping them into the first division in 1972.

ANDERSON, VIV. Defender Viv Anderson was a £250,000 signing from Nottingham Forest in July 1984. He spent just three seasons at Highbury, making 168 appearances, before becoming Alex Ferguson's first signing at Manchester United. Anderson had had a trial with United when he was a schoolboy but after being rejected had instead signed up with Nottingham Forest. It was at Forest that he was to enjoy his best days, especially once Brian Clough had begun to work his magic. He went on to make more

Viv Anderson

than 300 league appearances for Forest and picked up just about every honour in the game. He was a member of Forest's European Cup winning sides and won league championship and League Cup winners medals with Clough's side. He also won England honours at under-21 and B level and when he was chosen to represent England at full level in November 1978 he was the first black player to be capped by his country. He went on to win 30 England caps, 16 of these while he was at Arsenal. Anderson was a tall, leggy defender who preferred playing on the right side of defence. He also liked to get forward, scoring many valuable goals for his various clubs and country, including 16 for Arsenal. His only honour while at Highbury was a League Cup winners medal.

ANFIELD. The Liverpool ground was the scene of what was undoubtedly Arsenal's most dramatic victory. It came in injury time on 26 May 1989 when Michael Thomas swept into the Liverpool penalty area to score Arsenal's second goal and clinch the league championship for George Graham's young team.

APPEARANCES – LEAGUE. David O'Leary holds the record for the number of league appearances for Arsenal. Between 1975 and 1993 he played 558 games for the club.

ARMSTRONG, GEORGE. George Armstrong will be remembered as one of the Arsenal greats, not least for his record-breaking number of appearances. But, of course, there was much more to Armstrong. He was a workhorse in the Arsenal midfield, supplying so many of the chances that were eventually turned into goals and scoring more than a few himself. He joined the club in 1961 as a youngster, having been allowed to leave Newcastle and Grimsby after trials, and was soon competing for a place in the first team. He made his debut against Blackpool in February 1962 and then went on to give 17 seasons service. During that time he won just about every honour in the game, beginning with the Fairs Cup in 1970. A year later he picked up league and FA Cup medals. He also played in the 1968 and 1969 League Cup finals and the 1972 FA Cup final against Leeds United. He made his 500th and last league appearance for the club at Old Trafford on the final day of the 1976–77 season. In September of that year he moved to Leicester City and then had a spell with Stockport County before retiring in 1979. He was capped at England youth and under–23 level but, surprisingly, never went on to win a full cap for his country. By then wingers of his style were out of fashion with the England management. He eventually returned to Highbury to help coach the reserve side. In all, he played 713 games for Arsenal with a further 24 games as substitute, scoring 92 goals. For some time he held the record for the number of appearances for the club, until he was overtaken by David O'Leary.

ASHCROFT, JIMMY. Jimmy Ashcroft was the first Arsenal player to be capped by England. A goalkeeper, he won just three caps, keeping two clean sheets, but he was dropped after conceding a controversial goal against Scotland in 1906 when Jimmie Howie's powerful shot spun him round and the referee ruled that he had crossed the line while holding the ball. Scotland won 2–1 and he was never capped again. Ashcroft was born in Liverpool in 1878 and played with Everton as an amateur before moving south to join Gravesend United. After just one season he moved to Woolwich Arsenal in June 1900. Over the next eight seasons he was to miss only a handful of games and was said to be a fine, dependable goalkeeper. In May 1908 he was transferred to Blackburn Rovers and ended his playing days with Tranmere Rovers, then a non-league side. He made 390 appearances for the Gunners.

ATTENDANCE – HIGHEST. The record attendance at Highbury is 73,295, for a first division game against Sunderland on 9 March 1935. The game ended in a goalless draw.

B

BACUZZI, DAVE. Son of Joe Bacuzzi, the former Fulham defender. A full-back himself, Dave made his Arsenal debut in February 1961, but never really established himself. He played just 48 games before he was transferred to Manchester City in April 1964 for £25,000.

BAKER, ALF. An inter-war utility player who holds the distinction of having played in every position for Arsenal, including goal. He joined Arsenal in May 1919 after having played wartime football with Huddersfield Town. He made his league debut in August 1919 against Newcastle United and went on to represent Arsenal in just over 400 games. He even skippered the side for a while before handing the captaincy on to Charles Buchan. Baker played in the Cup final team which lost to Cardiff in 1927 but three years later he clinched his winners medal against Huddersfield Town. He was capped just once by England, in 1927 when he was almost 30 years of age, although he played in England trial games and twice for the Football League against the Irish League. Officially, he was an outside-left but he was happy to play anywhere as long as he was wearing a Gunners shirt. Many of his games were played as a full-back. Baker scored 40 goals for the club.

Joe Baker

BAKER, JOE. Liverpool-born Baker grew up in Scotland and, although he had an early trial with Chelsea, it was Hibernian who gave him his first chance in football, in 1957. International caps followed quickly and Baker became the first man to be capped by England while playing with a Scottish club. Within a few years he had scored 102 goals in 117 appearances in Scottish football and was soon snapped up by the Italian club Torino in the summer of 1961. But although he joined Denis Law there it was a deal that never really worked out. Baker was seriously injured in a car crash and a year later, pining for a return home, Billy Wright moved in with a record-breaking offer of £70,000. Baker made his debut for the Gunners against Leyton Orient in August 1962 and went on to play 186 games, scoring a remarkable 123 goals. He was an extra-ordinary striker, quick on the ball and deadly inside the six-yard box. He was soon back in the England side and pushing for a place in Alf Ramsey's World Cup squad, but with Jimmy Greaves and Roger Hunt also on the scene Baker was out of favour. It seemed to have a dramatic effect on him and his form slumped. In February 1966 he was transferred to Nottingham Forest for £65,000. He later played with Sunderland before returning to Hibernian. Baker was a great favourite with the Highbury crowd. At times he could be unpredictable but he was always a crowd-pleaser, an entertainer, and nobody could ever deny his prodigious talents.

BALDWIN, TOMMY. Baldwin's main claim to fame is that his transfer to Chelsea brought a young George Graham in the opposite direction, a move that was to dramatically transform the fortunes of Arsenal. Baldwin rose through the ranks of the Arsenal youth and reserve sides but played only 20 games before going to Chelsea, where at least he had more luck. His other claim to fame is in scoring Arsenal's first ever goal in the League Cup, when he netted against Gillingham in September 1966.

BALL, ALAN. The sale of Alan Ball by Everton came as a thunderbolt to Goodison supporters. Ball was one of the

Alan Ball

most popular players in the club's history, a man who had inspired England to World Cup glory and Everton to the league title. But suddenly, in December 1971, Evertonians awoke to read that their favourite had been sold to Arsenal for a British record fee of £220,000. Everton reckoned they had had the best out of him. How wrong could they be? Ball went on to play almost 250 games for Arsenal and then had a noteworthy spell with Southampton. Born in north Lancashire, Ball joined Blackpool in 1962 and had soon hit the headlines with his goalscoring feats. He was never an out-and-out goalscorer, but a playmaker. He was soon in the England reckoning, picking up his first cap in May 1965 against Yugoslavia when he was 19 years old. He was to win 14 caps over the next year, inspiring England to their famous World Cup triumph. By then he had played his last game for Blackpool and in the wake of England's victory he was transferred to Everton for £112,000. He won a further 39 caps at Everton before his dramatic transfer to Arsenal. Life at Highbury perhaps did not hold the glory that Ball had become accustomed to, as the club went through a period of transition. He did, however, pick up an FA Cup losers medal in 1972 against Leeds and was in the Arsenal side that were runners-up in the championship a year later. He also went on to win 33 more England caps. Ball may have been small and slight in appearance but he had the heart of a lion and the stamina of a tiger. He would harass, create opportunities, pass the ball with precision and could score goals just when they were most needed. He made 241 appearances for the Gunners and scored 57 goals before joining Southampton in December 1976.

BARGAIN BUYS. Arsenal have signed many players for a small fee who in time turned out to be bargains. Among them were goalkeeper Bob Wilson, signed from Wolves for just £5,000; Eddie Hapgood, who went on to captain Arsenal and England, bought by Herbert Chapman for £1,000 from Kettering in 1927; and Cliff Bastin, a £2,000 buy by Chapman from Exeter who went on to become the club's greatest goalscorer.

BARNES, WALLY. One of the greatest Arsenal players of the 1940s and 1950s. Barnes had played with Portsmouth and Southampton as an amateur before joining Arsenal in September 1943. He played in a number of wartime games for the Gunners but a knee injury in 1944 almost ended his career. He battled back from injury, however, and went on to play 335 games for the club. He made his debut for Arsenal against Preston North End in November 1946. Barnes was an outstanding defender, elegant but resolute, helping Arsenal to the league title in 1948 and the FA Cup in 1950. But he missed Arsenal's 1952–53 championship season after being seriously injured in the 1952 FA Cup final against Newcastle United. However, even that was not the end of Barnes, who came back yet again and continued playing until September 1955. He won his first international call-up, for Wales, during the war, winning his first official cap in 1947. He went on to collect 22 caps, his final game coming in 1954, making him at that time

Wally Barnes

Arsenal's most capped Welshman. Barnes was also captain of Arsenal and one of the most popular players of his generation. After he quit the game he became an adviser on football to BBC Television.

BARNETT, GEOFF. Joined Arsenal from Everton, where he had been understudy to Gordon West and Andy Rankin. Barnett cost £35,000 and began well, saving a penalty against Sporting Lisbon in the European Fairs Cup. Most of his time was spent as second-stringer to Bob Wilson and then Jimmy Rimmer, but he did appear in the 1972 FA. Cup final against Leeds United.

BARNWELL, JOHNNY. Another Bishop Auckland amateur who eventually found his way to the top with Arsenal. Barnwell joined the club in the mid–1950s but found the elegant Jimmy Bloomfield barring his progress. After Bloomfield had been sold he found himself winning a regular place in the side and even won England under–23 honours. He went on to play 151 games for the Gunners, scoring 24 goals, but eventually lost his place in 1964 and was transferred to Nottingham Forest. He also played with Sheffield United and found further fame as a manager with Peterborough, Wolves and AEK Athens, among others.

BARRON, PAUL. London-born goalkeeper of the late 1970s, Barron joined Arsenal from Plymouth Argyle but played only eight games before moving on to Crystal Palace. He later played with West Brom, Stoke and Queens Park Rangers.

BASTIN, CLIFF. The prodigy of his generation. Young Bastin made his debut for Exeter City at the age of 15, having already played for England schoolboys. At the age of 17 he joined Arsenal for £2,000 and a year later, in 1930, had picked up an FA Cup winners medal as the Gunners beat Huddersfield Town in the final. The following season he had a league championship medal and his first full England cap. By the time he retired he had won five championship medals, two FA Cup winners medals, 21 England caps and an FA Cup losers medal, to make him one of the most honoured players in the game. On top of that he also appeared in two wartime Cup finals. It was a remarkable career. Bastin was happy to play just about anywhere in attack, although he preferred the scheming role of inside-forward or to be out on the wing. In 425 games for Arsenal he managed 196 goals and his 150 goals in the league remains a record for the club. His first England cap came in November 1931 against Wales and his final cap seven years later in a 4–2 win over France. His 21 games for his country brought 12 goals. In his later playing career Bastin was hindered by increasing deafness. He remained with Arsenal throughout the war years but made only six more appearances after the war and finally quit the game in January 1947.

BATSON, BRENDON. West Indian born full-back with just four games to his credit. Batson left Arsenal in 1973 to join Cambridge United and then had a successful spell with West Bromwich Albion.

BENSON, BOB. Arsenal player who died while playing for the club. Born in Durham, Benson first played in 1903 with Newcastle United but a year later moved to Southampton. After just one season with the Southern League club he joined Sheffield United, where he was to remain for seven seasons, winning his one and only England cap, against Ireland in February 1913. Unfortunately, England lost. At the end of that season he joined Arsenal and played two seasons with them before war broke out. In that time he played 62 games at full-back, even scoring seven goals. During the war he was employed in munitions work and had little time for football, but in February 1916 he went to see Arsenal playing Reading at Highbury. The Arsenal side were a man short and Benson volunteered to play, even though he had not played for more than a year. During the game he was taken ill and was forced to leave the field. Later, in the dressing-room, he collapsed and died.

BLOCKLEY, JEFF. Blockley joined Arsenal from Coventry City in October 1972 for £200,000 as an intended replacement for skipper Frank McLintock. He began well and even made his England debut but he was never popular with the Highbury crowd or in the dressing-room, where there was much resentment that he should be replacing their captain. His form began to suffer and in May 1974, after 146 games, he was sold to Leicester City. His only England cap came in a 1–1 draw against Yugoslavia.

BLOOMFIELD, JIMMY. Had it not been for Jimmy Bloomfield's presence in what was a mediocre Arsenal side in the late 1950s, who knows where they might have ended up? Bloomfield saved his colleagues' lives on so many occasions with his authority and control. He was signed from Brentford by manager Tom Whittaker during the summer of 1954. Brentford had just been relegated to the third division and Bloomfield cost a mere £10,000. It was one of the best buys Whittaker would make. He spent seven seasons playing for the Gunners as an inside-forward, scoring 77 goals in his 291 outings. In 1957 he won two England under–23 caps and played for London against Barcelona in the 1958 Fairs Cup final. He also represented the Football League against the Scottish League but was never capped at full level by his country. When Arsenal signed George Eastham it marked the end of Bloomfield's days and he moved on to Birmingham City in November 1960 for £30,000, later playing with Brentford again as well as West Ham, Plymouth and Orient. He became manager at Orient and then enjoyed an even more successful spell managing Leicester City.

BLYTH, BILLY. Well-known Arsenal player of the 1920s. Blyth, born in Scotland, came to Arsenal via Manchester City, although he never made any appearances for City. He joined Arsenal in May 1914, making his debut against Huddersfield Town later that year. War had already broken out and he made only 12 appearances for the club before the war totally interrupted the league programme. After the war he became a regular in the side and was still young enough to give many seasons' service, playing a total of 389 games before he finally quit Highbury in 1929. During that time he had played in a Cup final, albeit on the losing side as Arsenal went down to Cardiff City. After Highbury he went to Birmingham, playing a further 21 games before he finally retired. He was a fine defender who lined up in a splendid Arsenal line alongside Jack Butler and Alf Baker.

BOOKS. Among the many books written on Arsenal are:
George Allison: *Allison Calling* (1934)
Herbert Chapman: *Herbert Chapman on Football* (1934)
Ralph Finn: *Arsenal, Chapman to Mee* (1969)
Nick Hornby: *Fever Pitch* (1992)
David Jack: *Soccer* (1934)
Stephen McGarrigle: *Green Gunners* (1991)
Geoffrey Mowbray: *Gunners on the Target* (1961)
Fred Ollier: *Arsenal, A Complete Record 1886–1988* (1988)
John Robertson: *Arsenal* (1985)
Phil Soar and Martin Tyler: *Arsenal* (1986)
Bob Wall: *Arsenal from the Heart* (1969)
Tom Watt: *The End* (1993)

BOULD, STEVE. Steve Bould's greatest moment probably came in the 1994 European Cup Winners Cup final when he played a Herculean role as Parma hurled everything at the Arsenal defence. But Bould matched his name in every aspect, standing firm in the eye of the hurricane. Although in the past he had often been ignored, he was singled out for special praise for his performance. He came to Arsenal from Stoke City for £390,000 during the summer of 1988 as an intended replacement for David O'Leary. But he did not have a comfortable ride at first. There were many who felt that O'Leary was being discarded far too soon and that Bould did not have the same sureness. Eventually they would be proved wrong but not before Bould had gone through a painful process of trying to convince the Highbury fans with some battling performances. Andy Linighan was also signed as a possible replacement but in the end

Steve Bould

Bould won the fans over to become a regular fixture in the back four. With a good first touch, Bould is an intelligent player who is considerably quicker than he looks. The honours have also come his way, with league championship medals in 1989 and 1991, although he missed out on Arsenal's 1993 Cup success because of a thigh injury. At 6 feet 4 inches he is a commanding presence in the Gunners defence and an admirable partner to Tony Adams.

BOWDEN, RAY. Another member of the great Arsenal side of the 1930s. Cornishman Bowden came to Highbury from Plymouth Argyle after helping them to the Third Division South championship. He joined Arsenal in March 1933 for £4,500 and went on to play a major role as Herbert Chapman's team took every honour in the game. He was a member of two league championship sides of 1934 and 1935, and won an FA Cup winners medal in 1936 as well as a Charity Shield medal in 1934. Bowden was more of an inside-forward than a centre-forward, netting 51 goals in his 144 appearances for the Gunners. He also picked up six England caps, the first against Wales in September 1934 and the last in December 1936 as England trounced Hungary 6–2. In November 1937 Bowden moved to Newcastle United for £5,000 but retired when war broke out.

BOWEN, DAVE. Welsh international wing-half who came to Arsenal in July 1950. He made his league debut against Wolves in March 1951 and went on to make more than 200 appearances for the club. He was a fine, dependable half-back who was a regular Welsh international even before he was a regular choice for the Gunners. He eventually won his place after the retirement of Joe Mercer and went on to become captain. Unfortunately, he did not play enough games to win a championship medal in 1953 and the rest of his Arsenal career was spent in a side that was going through change. He won a total of 19 caps for his country, captaining Wales in the 1958 World Cup finals when Wales came within a whisker of reaching the semifinals. In July 1959 he left Highbury to become player-manager of Northampton Town.

BOXING. Highbury has been an occasional venue for boxing over the years but never was it more in the spotlight than the night British Heavyweight Champion Henry Cooper took on the mighty Muhammad Ali for the World title. Unfortunately for London fight fans Muhammad Ali won the fight.

BRADSHAW, FRANK. Bradshaw was already a well-known player who had done the rounds of a number of league clubs before he joined Arsenal in June 1914. He had probably seen his best days with Sheffield Wednesday, where he won an FA Cup winners medal in the 1907 final as well as an England cap. His one and only England game was against Austria as England won 11–1, Bradshaw scoring a hat trick. He never played for his country again and so joined a list of just five players who have scored a hat trick in their one and only England game. Injury looked to have ended Bradshaw's career with Sheffield Wednesday in 1910 and he was transferred to Northampton Town in the Southern League, where his career was resurrected. A year later he went to Everton but it was not a particularly successful move as Everton finished in one of their lowest positions for years. Ironically, a season later they would be champions but by then Bradshaw had moved to Arsenal. He managed just one season before the war, but when it ended he converted from an attacking role to full-back and enjoyed a number of successful seasons, playing 164 games before retiring.

BRADSHAW, HARRY. Bradshaw was undoubtedly the first of the great Arsenal managers. He had begun in management with Burnley, coming to Arsenal in 1899 as successor to George Elcoat. Things were grim around Arsenal at that time but Bradshaw turned the club's fortunes around. New players were signed and the team finally won promotion in 1904. But just as the fans began to look forward to life in the first division Bradshaw sensationally resigned, tempted to Fulham by a big-money offer. It was a desperate loss for Arsenal, though it was something of a coup for

Fulham, who within five years went from the Southern League into the Football League and the semi-finals of the FA Cup.

BRADY, LIAM. Joined Arsenal as an apprentice and went on to become one of the club's great post-war stars. Born in Dublin, he was an Irish schoolboy international and went on to pick up 26 caps for the Republic while he was at Highbury and a further 46 after he had left. Brady was undoubtedly one of the most elegant midfielders in Europe: a hard tackler, a fine distributor of the ball and a man who could score goals as well as defend. He went on to play almost 350 games for the club, scoring 67 goals. During that time he appeared in three successive FA Cup finals as well as the European Cup Winners Cup final. But at the end of the day he had only one winners medal to show for all his endeavours. He was PFA Player of the Year in 1979. He made his debut for the club in October 1973, winning himself a regular place in the side during the 1974–75 season. During the summer of 1980 he decided to move to Italy, signing for Juventus. He also played with Sampdoria, Inter Milan and Ascoli, before returning to England to join West Ham United. During his time in Italy, Brady was

Liam Brady

widely regarded as one of the finest players ever imported from the English Football League. When he ended his playing days he became manager at Glasgow Celtic but it was an unhappy experience. He was later appointed manager of Brighton and Hove Albion. After he left, his presence in the Gunners midfield was sorely missed and it would be many years before any adequate replacement was unearthed. His loss was made all the more distressing by the fact that he went to Juventus for the knockdown price of £600,000, a bargain if ever there was one.

BRAIN, JIMMY. Prolific goalscorer of the 1920s, who for some years held the Arsenal goalscoring record. Born in Bristol in 1900, he joined Arsenal from Ton Pentre in August 1923. It was not long before he was in the first team and during the 1925–26 season hit 48 goals in 56 games, 34 of those coming in the league. He also played in an England trial that season but, with so much goalscoring talent in English football at the time, he was never selected to play for his country. Brain also played in the 1927 FA Cup final against Cardiff City, a club he was once on the books of as an amateur. In 1931 he won a league championship medal but then moved across north London to Tottenham Hotspur. He finally returned to Bristol, joining Bristol City, and eventually retired to become manager of Cheltenham Town. In 257 games for the Gunners he scored 159 goals.

BROWN, LAURIE. Central defender who joined Arsenal for £35,000 from Northampton Town in 1961. A northeasterner, he had played for Great Britain in the 1960 Rome Olympics while he was an amateur with Bishop Auckland. He went on to play just over 100 games for the Gunners before joining Tottenham Hotspur for £40,000 in February 1964. He was always a popular player at Highbury and after his time at Spurs he had spells with Norwich and Bradford Park Avenue.

BUCHAN, CHARLIE. One of the greatest names in the history of English football, yet a player who could have

Charlie Buchan

given so much more to Arsenal had the club been wise enough not to let him go as a youngster. Buchan was born in Plumstead and made four appearances for Woolwich Arsenal reserves before leaving the club after a row about expenses. He finally wound up at Leyton and a year later joined Sunderland, where he was to become one of the most prolific goalscorers of his era. As Sunderland clinched the championship in 1913 Buchan hit 27 goals but failed to find the net in the FA Cup final of that year as the Wearsiders missed out on the Double. In all, he scored 209 goals for Sunderland. He continued to play for them after the war but was signed by Herbert Chapman in 1925. He was then 33 years old and, although he was past his best, his contribution to the Arsenal cause was considerable. He was made captain and in his three seasons at Highbury Arsenal won the league championship and reached the FA Cup final. He played just 128 games for the club but scored 61 goals, a staggering number considering his age. He retired at the end of the 1927–28 season and his final game was at Goodison Park, where Everton clinched the title. More importantly, Dixie Dean needed three goals to break the Football League scoring record. Much to Buchan's annoyance Dean achieved his three goals, an event which totally overshadowed his retirement. For such an outstanding goalscorer it was surprising that Buchan was only capped six times by England. This was partly due to the war but was also largely due to the ineptitude of the England selectors, who seemed to be the only people who failed to recognise his goalscoring genius. When he retired he took up journalism, editing the famous *Charles Buchan's Football Monthly*.

BURNS, TONY. Goalkeeper who joined Arsenal from non-league Tonbridge United in March 1963. He made his debut against Enschede in Holland in August 1963 but did not make his league debut until 14 months later. Burns played just 26 games before handing over to Jim Furnell. In July 1966 he moved to Brighton.

BUTLER, JACK. The Baker/Butler/Blyth back line of the

1920s Arsenal side was one of the finest in the club's history and at the heart of it all was the towering Jack Butler. Butler joined Arsenal as a centre-forward just before the war and played many reserve-team games in that position. After the war, however, he converted to centre-half, becoming a regular in the side. He even won an England cap, playing against Belgium in England's 4–0 win. The change in the offside law in 1925, however, gave him a problem and in their first game that season Arsenal went down 0–7 to Newcastle. Manager Herbert Chapman reacted by pulling Butler further back to make him into a central defender. In effect he was the first 'stopper' in English football. But it was a masterstroke by Chapman. Butler continued to play for the Arsenal for many more years, winning a losers medal in the 1927 Cup final against Cardiff. In 1930 he was transferred to Torquay United for £1,000 but retired a couple of seasons later. Ironically, he then went on to coach the Belgium national side and later had spells as a coach with Leicester and as manager at Torquay, Crystal Palace and Colchester. He made 335 appearances for the Gunners, scoring 11 goals.

C

CAESAR, GUS. Gus Caesar exploded on to the Arsenal scene only to slowly fizzle out. The Tottenham-born youngster came through the Highbury ranks, making his debut at Old Trafford at right-back with a dazzling performance. Within a couple of years he had won three England under-21 caps and looked set for a long-term future with the club. But he could never quite establish himself in the side. Admittedly, he broke an ankle three times, but his performances seemed to lack commitment. Against Luton Town in the 1988 Littlewoods Cup final he made the error that cost Arsenal the lead, and probably the match as well. After that it was downhill all the way, especially once Andy Linighan had been recruited. At the end of the 1990–91 season he was given a free transfer and went to Cambridge United. After a couple of months they let him go and he finished up at Bristol City. But even that did not last and he was soon on his way to Scotland, joining Airdrieonians.

CAMPBELL, KEVIN. Another of the many South London-born youngsters who came to first-team football through the junior and reserve-team ranks at Highbury. He had a loan spell with Leyton Orient and Leicester City, where he gained valuable experience and netted a healthy tally of goals. George Graham was somewhat slow in giving him a chance of regular first-team football but eventually it came and he has now become a firm fixture in the Arsenal side. He won championship honours and then an FA Cup winners medal in 1993 on top of the League Cup medal he had won a few months earlier. In 1994 he added a European Cup Winners medal to make him one of the most honoured young players in British football. Campbell is a strong, fast, attacking forward, eager to get into penalty areas and with a sharp turn and ability to shoot. He looks set to spend many more years at Highbury though he has yet to prove his full potential.

CAPACITY. The total capacity of Highbury in 1994, after the completion of its redevelopment into an all-seater stadium, is 39,000. The club's highest attendance is 73,295, recorded against Sunderland in a division one game on 9 March 1935.

CAPTAINS. Among the many players who have captained the club since the Second World War have been Joe Mercer, Wally Barnes, Dave Bowen, Frank McLintock, Graham Rix, Kenny Sansom and Tony Adams.

CARTER, JIMMY. There was some surprise when manager George Graham paid Liverpool £500,000 for young winger Jimmy Carter. Carter had originally been with Millwall but had been signed by Kenny Dalglish for £800,000 towards the end of his reign at Anfield. Carter played only a handful of games for Liverpool, never really looking the part, and was then sold by new manager Graeme Souness to Arsenal. But it was a deal that never really worked out for Arsenal and in 1994 Carter was loaned to Oxford United.

CATON, TOMMY. Joined Arsenal from Manchester City in December 1983 for £500,000 after impressing many with his powerful performances in the heart of the City defence. He had also captained the England under-21 side and looked a particularly bright prospect. Unfortunately, Caton never looked the part at Highbury and lasted only two seasons. The tall, blond-haired Caton played just 95 games and was then transferred to Oxford United. He later played with Charlton Athletic but died of a heart-attack at a tragically early age.

CENTENARY. Arsenal celebrated their centenary in 1986.

CHAMPIONSHIP. See League Championship.

CHAPMAN, HERBERT. Perhaps the greatest manager the English game has ever known; a man whose vision and ideas helped make English football so envied and Arsenal Football Club one of the greatest names in world soccer. Chapman was born near Sheffield in January 1878. His footballing career, however, was hardly in the highest bracket. He played with a number of non-league clubs and he even had spells with Tottenham Hotspur and Northampton Town. In 1907 he was appointed player-manager of Northampton, and took them to the Southern League title in 1909 in only his second season. He then went to Leeds City, where he again began to have some success, but after a League inquiry concerning financial irregularities at Leeds the club was closed down in 1919. Chapman was not involved but, finding himself out of a job, he returned to his old occupation as a mining engineer. However, it was not long before Huddersfield Town stepped in and appointed him manager. Chapman was on his way and in a five-year spell at Leeds Road he took Huddersfield into the first division and won the FA Cup and two successive league titles before applying for the post of manager at Arsenal. At the time, Arsenal were hovering in the lower reaches of the first division but Chapman had plans, spending heavily to bring in players such as Charlie Buchan, Joe Hulme, Tom Parker and Jack Lambert. The magic soon began to work and when Cliff Bastin, David Jack, Eddie Hapgood and others were added to the squad the honours began to pour in. In 1930 they won the FA Cup, beating Chapman's old side Huddersfield Town in the final. A year later they won the league title. The following season they were runners-up in the league and reached the FA Cup

Herbert Chapman

final only to lose to Newcastle. The following season they won the league title again, the first of three successive championships. Then at the end of 1934, after watching a midweek game, he caught a chill. It developed into pneumonia and as thousands of Arsenal fans poured into Highbury on Saturday, 6 January they learned that their manager had died. He was only 59 years old. Chapman's achievements were considerable. Not only did he turn Arsenal into such a great force but he also pioneered many changes in the game: he had floodlights installed at Highbury for training purposes and was involved in the numbering of players' shirts and the construction of new stands that made Highbury the finest ground in the country, improving spectator facilities and arguing for the Gillespie Road tube station to be renamed Arsenal. Chapman was a giant among managers, unquestionably the man who created the modern Arsenal.

CHAPMAN, LEE. The much-travelled Lee Chapman was barely given a chance at Highbury. At £500,000 he was a costly buy from Stoke City for manager Terry Neill, but he lasted less than 18 months before he was sold to Sunderland for £100,000. He had played only 17 games. He began well enough but was soon injured and never recovered enough to impress the Arsenal fans. He had been bought as a replacement for the popular Frank Stapleton and never lived up to the role. Instead of persevering, Neill decided to sell him. After Sunderland he had spells with Sheffield Wednesday, Niort of France, Nottingham Forest and then Leeds United. At Forest his career began to blossom and came into full bloom at Elland Road, where he helped Leeds to the championship.

CHARITY SHIELD. Arsenal have appeared in the Charity Shield on 13 occasions, winning the pre-season friendly seven times:
1930 v Sheffield Wednesday (Stamford Bridge) 2–1
1931 v WBA (Villa Park) 1–0
1933 v Everton (Goodison Park) 3–0
1934 v Manchester City (Highbury) 4–0
1935 v Sheffield Wednesday (Highbury) 0–1
1936 v Sunderland (Roker Park) 1–2
1938 v Preston North End (Highbury) 2–1
1948 v Manchester United (Highbury) 4–3
1953 v Blackpool (Highbury) 3–1
1979 v Liverpool (Wembley) 1–3
1989 v Liverpool (Wembley) 0–1
1991 v Tottenham (Wembley) 0–0
1993 v Manchester United (Wembley) 1–1 Manchester

United won on penalties
After the draw against Tottenham in 1991, the
trophy was shared.

CHARLES, MEL. Brother of the great John Charles, Mel
was also a Welsh international, winning a total of 31 caps
for his country. He signed for Arsenal in March 1959 for
£42,750 plus a couple of Arsenal reserve players. It was a
huge deal although it fell considerably short of the £70,000
Juventus had paid Leeds United for his brother. Mel had
also had trials with Leeds but drifted back to Wales, joining
Swansea in May 1952. He made well over 200 appearances
for the Welsh club, scoring 69 goals and winning 21 caps for
his country. That brought him to the attention of Arsenal
but it was not to be a particularly happy period for him.
No sooner had he pulled on an Arsenal shirt than he was
injured, needing a cartilage operation. He returned, eventually making 25 appearances in the 1959–60 season but
then needed a second operation. He made just 19 league
appearances in the 1960–61 season and then struggled to
find a place in the side. Although he was never in the same
class as his brother, he was equally adept, able to play
at centre-half, centre-forward or half-back. He was tall,
powerful and promised so much but luck seemed to con-
spire against him and in the end his Highbury career turned
out to be something of a disappointment. After less than
100 games and 37 goals, he returned to Wales in February
1962, joining Cardiff City for £28,500. During his Arsenal
days he picked up a further six caps.

CHARLTON, STAN. 1950s defender not renowned for his
subtlety. Charlton was a committed full-back – committed
to getting the ball at all costs. Often he did, but just as
often he could be left standing. Charlton had been a famous
amateur in his early days, playing in the Great Britain side
at the 1952 Olympic Games. At the time he was with Leyton
Orient but joined Arsenal in November 1955 in a deal that
also brought Vic Groves to Highbury. He went on to play
110 games over the next three seasons before returning to
Leyton Orient, where he put in another six years.

Mel Charles

CLAMP, EDDIE. Clamp was one of the most feared defenders in the game when he was at Wolverhampton Wanderers. He had starred in a Wolves side that had won many honours and that boasted as fine a half-back line as any in the world. Indeed, it was so good that it was also the England half-back line in the 1958 World Cup finals. Clamp won his first England cap in the finals and his fourth cap a month later as England drew with Austria. He was signed by George Swindin in November 1961 for £34,500 to add some bite to the Arsenal defence. But when Billy Wright took over from Swindin a short time later it spelled the end of Eddie Clamp. Wright was said not to be keen on Clamp's ferocious tackling, but considering they had played alongside one another for so many years at Wolves his disapproval seems odd. More likely there was bad blood between the two. Clamp remained at Arsenal for just ten months before Wright sold him to Stoke City for less than half what Arsenal had paid for him. He had played only four games under Wright.

CLAPTON, DANNY. Winger Danny Clapton was one of those players who never quite fulfilled his potential. Perhaps in a better Arsenal team he might have matured into an outstanding player. As it was, there were only mere hints of promise. He joined the Gunners in 1953 following a trial, making his league debut on Christmas Day 1954 against Chelsea. He quickly became a star in a very drab Arsenal side, winning his one and only England cap in 1958 against Wales. He was the first Gunner to be capped by England in five years. Clapton was a clever winger, with a neat body swerve and plenty of pace. But he always needed encouragement and hated physical defenders who could so easily snuff him out of the game. One good whack and that was it; Clapton would shrink on to the touchline for the rest of the afternoon. He played almost 300 games for the club, scoring just 38 goals – perhaps not as many as might have been expected from a winger. Clapton played for the Football League against the Irish League in 1958 but in September 1962 he quit Highbury to join Luton Town.

COACH. The current Arsenal coach is Stewart Houston. The reserve-team coach is George Armstrong and the youth coach is Pat Rice. Well-known Arsenal coaches of the past have included, among others, Don Howe, Dave Sexton and Leslie Compton.

COCA-COLA CUP. See Football League Cup.

COLE, ANDY. All managers can make mistakes and Andy Cole will always figure among George Graham's nightmares. With Ian Wright and Alan Smith at Highbury, Graham decided that he had enough goalscorers and let the young Cole go to Bristol City for £500,000. At the time it seemed a wise decision. Cole did well at Bristol but soon moved on to Newcastle United where he began to develop into a spectacular goalscorer. He went on to break the club's goalscoring record, hitting 40 goals, to make him the leading goalscorer in the Premiership for 1993–94.

COLEMAN, ERNEST 'TIM'. Played for Halifax and Grimsby Town before joining Arsenal in March 1932 for £7,500. His 57 goals in 85 appearances for Grimsby had helped them into the first division and brought his name to the attention of most of the big clubs. In his first full season at Highbury, 1932–33, Coleman won a league championship medal, scoring 24 goals in 27 league appearances. The following season he was in and out of the side as the goals failed to materialise. When Arsenal then signed Ted Drake he decided, probably wisely, that his days were numbered at Highbury and promptly signed for Middlesbrough. He later went to Norwich before war intervened to end his playing career. After the war he had a spell as manager of Notts County. He played a total of 53 games for the Gunners, scoring 31 goals, but the nearest he came to international honours was an England trial game.

COLEMAN, JOHN GEORGE 'TIM'. Inside-forward of the 1900s. Coleman played his early football in the Southern League with Kettering and then Northampton Town. He came to Arsenal in May 1902 and went on to play 42 games the following season, scoring 24 goals. Coleman was a prolific scorer for an inside-forward, hitting a total of 110 goals in 237 games for the club. His best season was 1903–4, when he struck 23 league goals in just 28 appearances as Arsenal won promotion from the second division. He won just one England cap, in February 1907, when he played against Ireland at Goodison Park. He also played in five England trial matches and twice appeared for the Football League. During the summer of 1908 he was transferred to Everton and later played with Sunderland, Fulham and Nottingham Forest before coaching in Holland.

COLOURS. During their early years Arsenal played in all-red shirts. Their first set of shirts was given to them by Nottingham Forest, some of their founder members having played for Forest. In 1895 they briefly changed to red and light blue vertically striped shirts. Up until the late 1930s they continued to play in red shirts and white shorts but then changed their colours to red shirts with white sleeves, white shorts and red stockings – colours they have maintained ever since. Arsenal's present away colours are yellow shirts and navy shorts with yellow stockings.

COMMON, ALF. The first player to break the £1,000 transfer barrier, when he joined Middlesbrough from Sunderland in February 1905. He had also been the first player to smash the £500 barrier. Prior to playing with those two clubs, Common had starred with Sheffield United, winning an FA Cup winners medal in 1902 and a couple of England caps. He joined Woolwich Arsenal in August 1910 from Middlesbrough after helping keep the Teeside club in the first division. But it was not the happiest of periods for Arsenal and he lasted just a couple of seasons. He left halfway through his third season as results went from bad to worse. In all, he played 91 games for the club, scoring 29 goals. An out-and-out goalscorer, his best season had been 1911–12, when he struck 17 league goals in 36 outings. He then moved to second-division Preston, where he was luckier, helping them into the first division. Common won just three England caps, scoring three goals.

COMPTON, DENIS. Every post-war English schoolboy's hero and one of the great names of English cricket and Arsenal Football Club. Compton was born in Hendon in north London in 1918. After winning schoolboy international honours with England at football, he joined Arsenal as an amateur in September 1932. He turned professional three years later but did not make his league debut for the club until September 1936, when he also scored as Arsenal drew 2–2 with Derby County at Highbury. Compton was never really a regular in the Arsenal side, though had war not interrupted his career he might well have gone on to concentrate on his more demanding football career. He played in two wartime Cup finals and picked up 12 wartime caps. But by the time war came to an end his cricket career was blossoming and his best footballing days were behind him. But he still went on to win a league championship medal in 1948 and an FA Cup winners medal in 1950 as Arsenal beat Liverpool at Wembley. He was never capped as a full England international. After the 1950 Cup final he quit the game to concentrate on his cricket. He had played 79 games for the club, scoring 24 goals.

COMPTON, LESLIE. Older brother of Denis Compton and another famous Arsenal footballer/cricketer. Born in Woodford in Essex in September 1912, Compton first played with Hampstead Town before joining Arsenal as an amateur. He turned professional in February 1932 and made his league debut two months later against Aston Villa. He was then a full-back but with so much competition for places at the back it was to be some years before he became a regular. Right up until the war his opportunities were limited and he made only 67 appearances in eight seasons. During the war, however, he began to come into his own as he converted to centre-forward, often scoring at a prolific rate. Against Clapton Orient in a London wartime Cup game he even scored ten goals as Arsenal thrashed Clapton 15–2. He also won five England wartime caps but after the war he changed position again, this time to centre-half, the position he was to become most closely associated with. He was a member of the Arsenal side that won the league championship in 1948 and then won a Cup winners medal in 1950, playing alongside his brother. In that same year he won the first of his two England caps when he played against Wales. He was, at the age of 38, the oldest player ever to make his debut for England. He won a second cap a week later as England drew with Yugoslavia, one of the Yugoslav goals, unfortunately, coming from Compton. It was to be the last time he would play for his country. In 1952 he retired from the game but took up a coaching position at Highbury. Like his brother Denis, he also played county cricket for Middlesex but was never selected to play for England. His Arsenal playing career had spanned 21 years with 332 appearances and ten goals.

COPPING, WILF. Copping, like so many Barnsley men before him, was something of a hard man. He was renowned for his tough tackling but went on to win England honours and was one of the finest wing-halves in Arsenal's history. He had trials with his home team, Barnsley, but was rejected. Instead, he joined Leeds United in 1930 and after almost 160 league outings signed for Arsenal for £8,000 in June 1934. He was already an England international with six caps to his name and was now joining England's top club. The rest of the Football League must have shuddered at the prospect. Copping went on to win two league championship medals, an FA Cup winners medal and played in two winning Charity Shield sides. He also went on to win 13 more England caps while he was at Highbury, his most memorable as England, or rather Arsenal, beat the World Cup holders Italy at Highbury. After just over 200 games for Arsenal, Copping made a surprise return to Leeds in March 1939, making one more England appearance before war broke out and effectively ended his career. By the time it was over he was too old, and settled instead to coach, spending a period as coach of the Belgian national side before enjoying spells with Southend, Bristol City and Coventry.

CORONATION CUP. Arsenal, along with Celtic, Rangers, Aberdeen, Hibernian, Newcastle, Manchester United and

Tottenham Hotspur, competed for the Coronation Cup in 1953. The competition was held in Scotland with Arsenal going out after their first game, a 0–1 defeat by Celtic watched by a crowd of more than 59,000. Arsenal had just won the league championship.

COURT, DAVID. Made his debut for Arsenal as an 18-year-old in September 1962 and, after starring against Spurs with a couple of goals, it seemed that Arsenal had found a gem. But it was not to be, as his early form soon evaporated. Billy Wright gave him a second chance by converting him into a half-back and he went on to pick up losers medals in the League Cup finals of 1968 and 1969, playing almost 200 games and scoring ten goals. He played with Luton Town and Brentford after his days with Arsenal.

COX, FREDDIE. Formerly a Spurs player, Cox came to Highbury in September 1949. He was born in Reading, joining Tottenham as a professional just a year before the outbreak of war. He had little chance to establish himself before the war but when hostilities came to an end he went on to make 89 appearances for Spurs before his transfer to Arsenal. Cox's most memorable performances came in the 1950 and 1952 FA Cup semi-finals when he scored on both occasions, against Chelsea, to give the Gunners a place at Wembley. Cox went on to pick up a winners medal in the 1950 final and a losers medal two years later. He made just over 100 appearances for Arsenal before leaving to join West Bromwich Albion as player-coach. He later became assistant manager at the Hawthorns and subsequently had spells as manager of Bournemouth, Portsmouth, Gillingham and Bournemouth again.

CRAWFORD, GAVIN. One of Arsenal's first ever professionals. Born in Scotland, he came to Arsenal via Sheffield United in the summer of 1891. Crawford played in Royal Arsenal's pre-league games and then in 1893 made his league debut as Arsenal joined the Football League. He went on to play a total of 329 games for the club, scoring 77 goals and was captain for several years. In the summer of 1898 he moved to Millwall and later played with Queens Park Rangers.

CRAYSTON, JACK. Player and manager. One of the most eminent wing-halves ever to play for the Gunners. Crayston began his footballing days with his local club, Barrow, but in 1930 moved to Bradford, where he made almost 100 appearances before Arsenal moved in with a £5,250 offer for his services in May 1934. It was a substantial fee in those days but Crayston more than justified Arsenal's outlay. He went on to make over 200 appearances for the club, scoring 21 goals and collecting every honour in the game. In 1934–35 he won a league championship medal and a year later an FA Cup winners medal. In 1935 he won the first of eight international caps when he starred in England's 3–0 win over Germany. He also played in the FA Charity Shield but the outbreak of war was to bring his career to an end. After the war he joined the Highbury coaching staff, becoming assistant manager and then manager in November 1956 after the death of Tom Whittaker. But it was not a happy period, either for Crayston or Arsenal. They were 11th in the league when he took over and went on to finish in fifth spot with a sixth-round appearance in the FA Cup. That was fine but the following season everything began to go wrong. The club would not give him money to buy new players as form slumped and Arsenal consequently finished the season in 12th place with their lowest points tally since 1930. To makes matters even worse, they were knocked out of the FA Cup by Northampton. It marked the end of Crayston's days. He pleaded with the board for more cash but none was forthcoming and in May 1958 he resigned. Within a few months he was back in football, managing Doncaster Rovers, but after three years left to run a newsagent's business near Birmingham.

CRICKET. A number of Arsenal players have also played first-class cricket. The most famous were undoubtedly the Compton brothers. Others include Andy Ducat, who won six caps for the England football side as well as playing in one Test match, against Australia at Headingley in 1921. By then Ducat was an Aston Villa player. He also played county cricket for Surrey for 25 years and died of a heart-attack while batting at Lords. Wally Hardinge was another who played for England at both cricket and soccer, though he was not an Arsenal player when he won his football cap. Arthur Milton, who played against Austria in 1951, was the last player to be capped by England at cricket and football. Among the many other Arsenal men who played first-class cricket were Joe Hulme, Ted Drake, Don Roper, Jim Standen, Harry Storer, Ray Swallow and George Cox. Cricketing honours have not been restricted to the dressing-rooms either, with two Arsenal chairmen – Samuel Hill-Wood and Denis Hill-Wood – both playing for Derbyshire.

CROPLEY, ALEX. A £150,000 signing by Bertie Mee from Hibernian in December 1974. Cropley was the golden boy of Scottish football, a Scottish international and a player high on everyone's shopping list. Much was expected of Cropley, a tough but elegant defender, but while he might have been well equipped for Scottish football he was far less prepared for the physical nature of the English game. Cropley was a lightweight playing in a heavyweight division and it was not long before the inevitable consequences of his game struck in the form of injury. He broke a leg not long after he arrived and missed the rest of the season. He then returned but not for long before injury struck again. And so it went on. Eventually, in September 1976, Bertie Mee gave up on him and sold him to Aston Villa for £135,000. He had played only 33 games for the Gunners. He had some success with Villa, helping them to a League Cup triumph, but more injuries and an inevitable early retirement followed.

D

DANIEL, RAY. Arsenal defender of the post-war years. Daniel joined Arsenal as an amateur immediately after the war, having also played with Swansea as an amateur. National service, however, postponed his debut for some years. It finally came against Charlton Athletic in May 1949. He then went on to play 123 games for the Gunners, mainly at centre-half, following the retirement of Les Compton. But it was not until the 1951–52 season that he really established himself as a regular. He won an FA Cup runners-up medal in 1952, playing with his arm in plaster. The following season he won a league championship medal but was then surprisingly sold at the end of the season to Sunderland for £27,500. He was later suspended at Sunderland for receiving illegal payments and in 1957 moved to Cardiff City but played only a handful of games for them before returning to his first club, Swansea. He won his first Welsh cap while he was still a reserve player with Arsenal in 1950, against England, and went on to win 12 caps while he was at Highbury. Daniel also served as player-manager of Hereford Town.

DAVIS, PAUL. One of many Arsenal youngsters reared through the ranks and who came to the fore under manager

George Graham. South London-born Davis made his debut against Tottenham Hotspur in April 1980. He soon won a regular spot in the team and went on to pick up England under-21 honours. He played a major part in the 1986–87 season as Arsenal lifted the League Cup and then continued his rise with some fine performances as Arsenal went on to win league championship honours in 1989 and 1991. But it has not all been glowing success. There were moments when he faded and was dropped but he always showed commitment and application, making an eventual return to the side. He spent a year on the sidelines, returning to first-team action in March 1992 to add two more medals to his collection with his FA Cup and League Cup winners medals in 1993. He also starred in Arsenal's European Cup Winners Cup triumph in 1994. Davis was the first black player to really make it at Highbury and has become a role model for a whole generation of young black players at the club.

DEFEAT – WORST. Arsenal's record defeat was when Loughborough beat them 8–0 in a second division game in December 1896.

DEFEATS – FEWEST. During the 1990–91 season Arsenal lost just one game – and that was away from home. This is a record for the first division in modern times.

DEFEATS – MOST. Arsenal have twice lost a total of 23 games in a season. In 1912–13 they lost 10 games at home and 13 games away and were subsequently relegated. Then in the 1924–25 season they lost six games at home and 17 games away. On this occasion they avoided relegation and the following season they were runners-up.

DEFENSIVE RECORD – BEST. Arsenal won the 1990–91 championship conceding a mere 19 goals in 38 games.

DEFENSIVE RECORD – WORST. Arsenal's worst defensive record was in seasons 1926–27 and 1927–28. In each season they conceded 86 goals.

DERBYS. The first Arsenal-Tottenham league derby took place on 16 December 1909. It was a first division game, won by Arsenal 1–0. The two clubs had, however, played each other in friendly and Cup games prior to this date. The first ever game between the two clubs was played on 19 November 1887 with Royal Arsenal losing 1–2 at Tottenham in a friendly. The game was abandoned after 75 minutes because of bad light.

DEVINE, JOHN. Joined Arsenal along with David O'Leary but never enjoyed anything like the success of his fellow Irishman. Devine fitted into the right-back slot after the departure of Pat Rice and made a promising start, but progress never followed. He won his first Irish cap in 1979 against Czechoslovakia. He went on to collect seven caps while he was at Highbury and then picked up a further five while he was with Norwich. He joined Norwich on a free transfer in 1983 and later moved to Stoke until a broken leg ended his career.

DIAL SQUARE. The first name that Arsenal ever played under in 1886.

DICK, JOHN. John Dick had an astonishing record for Arsenal, playing more than 400 games over a 12-year period. Born in Scotland, he joined Arsenal in 1898, having played with Airdrieonians, and for the next seven seasons he barely missed a game. He could play anywhere across the half-back line and was team captain for many years. Yet, despite his consistency and undoubted ability, his only honour was to captain the side which won promotion in 1904. When he retired from playing in 1910 he took up a coaching position with the club and two years later was appointed coach to the Prague Deutscher club in Czechoslovakia. He later held a similar position with Sparta Prague.

DIXON, LEE. Manchester-born Lee Dixon began his career with Burnley but looked to have little future in the game as the Lancashire club gave him a free transfer. He went to Chester and then to Bury for £3,500 where he suddenly began to show signs of improvement, tempting second division Stoke City to pay £40,000 for him. That was in 1986. Two years later, in January 1988, George Graham was paying ten times that amount and the young full-back was well and truly on his way. Within a couple of seasons he would be an England international and the owner of a bagful of medals. He won league championship honours in 1989 and 1991, an FA Cup winners medal in 1993 and a European Cup Winners Cup medal in 1994 after giving a magnificent display against Parma. He won his first England cap in 1990 against Czechoslovakia and within a couple of years had already picked up 20 caps, laying claim to the right-back slot. Dixon is a sturdy defender with an impressive turn of pace and, like many modern full-backs, he likes to get forward and work his way into the penalty area. He also has a fine, accurate cross and when he takes the ball to the line can prove to be exceptionally dangerous.

DOCHERTY, TOMMY. Docherty joined Arsenal at the back end of his footballing career, when he was recruited from Preston North End in the summer of 1958 for £27,000. He made his debut in an Arsenal shirt against Burnley in August of that year and went on to make 90 appearances over the next three years. Docherty had been an attacking wing-half but at Highbury he assumed more defensive responsibilities, bringing some much-needed organisation to the Gunners defence. From mid-table mediocrity Arsenal were soon challenging the league leaders but a broken ankle for Docherty in the autumn of 1959 put paid to any hopes the Gunners might have been harbouring for a serious title assault. In 1961, past his most influential as a player, Docherty transferred his talents to the coaching side and accepted a job with Chelsea. It was the beginning of a new chapter in his life, if not an entire book, and over the next couple of decades he would manage a host of clubs, including Chelsea, QPR, Scotland, Manchester United, Oporto and Derby County, among others. Docherty won three Scottish caps while he was with Arsenal to add to the 22 he won while he was with Preston.

Tommy Docherty

DOCTORS. The only time you might expect to see a doctor on the pitch is when someone is injured, yet Arsenal can boast four doctors who actually played professional football for them. They were Kevin O'Flanagan, Leigh Roose, James Paterson and James Marshall.

DODGIN, BILL. Started out as a centre-half at Fulham, where his father was the manager, and joined Arsenal in 1953 as a replacement for Ray Daniel. He began well enough, even captaining the England under–23 side, but then seemed to lose his way. He nevertheless went on to play just over 200 games for the club. Dodgin had his critics but he was always committed and battled for his place. Eventually, Mel Charles arrived and Dodgin took the hint and moved back to Fulham. He later had spells as a manager with Queens Park Rangers, Fulham, Northampton and Brentford.

DOUBLE. In 1971 Arsenal became only the second club this century to clinch the coveted league and FA Cup double. In their final league match they defeated Tottenham at White Hart Lane to win the league title and then, a few days later, beat Liverpool at Wembley to clinch the Double. The only other double which Arsenal have achieved was to win the FA Cup and the League Cup in the same season. That was in 1993, when they beat Sheffield Wednesday in both competitions.

DRAKE, TED. Of all the great strikers to have worn the Arsenal colours, Ted Drake is perhaps the greatest. Drake will always be remembered for the seven goals he struck against Aston Villa at Villa Park in December 1935. Arsenal won 7–1 that day and Drake's seven goals equalled the long-standing first division record for the most goals in a game. The previous season he had also set the Arsenal record for the highest number of goals in a season as he scored 42 in 41 appearances, a record which still stands. Drake was born in Southampton in 1912, joining his home-town club in 1931. He immediately continued the goalscoring feats he had started as a schoolboy, netting 48 goals in

72 games before Arsenal snapped him up for £6,500 in March 1934. A season later he was rewriting the High-bury goalscoring record book as well. Drake's career at Arsenal continued unabated. He scored the only goal of the 1936 Cup final and won two league championship medals, plus two Charity Shield medals. He picked up his first England cap at the age of 22 against Italy at Highbury in the famous match when seven Arsenal players lined up against the Italians. He even scored that day. Well he would at Highbury, wouldn't he! Drake went on to win five England caps, scoring six goals, though it is surprising that he did not win more. During the war he injured his spine playing for Reading and it effectively ended his playing career. He had enjoyed just six seasons with Arsenal, making 197 appearances and scoring an astonishing 150 goals. At the end of the war he became manager at Reading and then joined Chelsea as manager in 1952, guiding them to the first league championship in their history, in 1955. He left Chelsea in 1961 and became a director of Fulham.

DUCAT, ANDY. Double England international of the Edwardian era. Ducat was born in Surrey in 1886 and joined Woolwich Arsenal as an amateur in January 1905. Over the next eight seasons he was to play 213 games for the club, scoring 30 goals, a not inconsiderable number for a half-back. Ducat had once been a centre-forward and delighted at the prospect of getting into the goalmouth. He won his first England cap against Ireland in 1910 and his second against Wales the same year, when he scored the only goal of the game. After his third cap, again awarded in 1910, he had to wait nine years before he was selected again. For many years this stood as a record. He went on to win six caps, the last in October 1920. Strapped for cash, Arsenal were forced to sell Ducat to Aston Villa for £1,000 in June 1912. At Villa his career brought him even more honours, including an FA Cup winners medal in 1920 when he skippered Villa to success against Huddersfield Town. It made up for having missed Villa's 1913 Cup final side with a broken leg. But Ducat was also known as a fine cricketer. He played for Surrey for 25 years between 1906 and 1931 and appeared in one Test match for England, against Australia at Leeds in 1921. He was out in a most unusual manner in that game as the ball chipped a chunk of wood off his bat and on to his stumps. After Villa, Ducat took over as manager at Fulham. He was later coach at Eton College and died of a heart-attack while playing cricket at Lords.

E

EASTHAM, GEORGE. With George Eastham and Joe Baker playing alongside each other during the early 1960s, Arsenal boasted two of the most elegant players in the Football League. Some have even called Eastham one of the finest play-makers in Arsenal's history. Eastham came to Highbury following a court battle over the right of players to be transferred. It had been a prolonged case that was eventually to have major consequences as the old slave system came to an abrupt end. Eastham cost Arsenal a huge £47,500 in November 1960 when he signed from Newcastle United but the publicity surrounding his legal battle was to have an effect on his game and it was some time before he began to show the kind of form that had made him a target for Arsenal. Eventually, he began to shine. He was a superb passer of the ball and had a delicate touch that could baffle defenders. He won his first England cap in the 1–1 draw with Brazil in May 1963. His father, George senior, had been an international in 1935 when he was with Bolton Wanderers and George junior's cap meant that they were the first father and son to play for England. George junior went on to win a total of 19 caps for England, winning his final cap immediately prior to the World Cup finals. Although he was a member of the England squad

George Eastham

for the finals, he was unfortunate not to play in any of the games. Of slight build, he always looked likely to be blown away by any robust defender. But he had stamina and strength way beyond his size. He played a total of 267 games for the club, scoring 66 goals before Arsenal sold him in August 1966 to Stoke City, where his career took on a new lease of life. He won a League Cup winners medal with Stoke in 1972 and went on to become manager.

EIRE. The first Arsenal player to be capped by the Republic of Ireland was Jimmy Dunne, when he played against Switzerland in 1936. International or not, he only played 30-odd games for the Gunners. The most capped Irish player in Arsenal's history is David O'Leary, who has won a total of 67 caps. Other outstanding Irish internationals from Highbury have included Liam Brady and Frank Stapleton.

ELCOAT, GEORGE. Arsenal manager between 1898 and

1899. Born in Stockton-on-Tees, Elcoat had only a short period in charge of team affairs. He particularly liked Scottish players and during his time there were no less than eight Scots playing in the side. But these were bad times for Arsenal and as matters slid from bad to worse, with players being offloaded to save on wages, Elcoat resigned.

ENGLAND. The first Arsenal player ever to be capped by England was goalkeeper Jimmy Ashcroft, who played for England against Northern Ireland in 1906. England won 5–0. The Arsenal player to win the most England caps is Kenny Sansom, who made 77 appearances for his country while an Arsenal player. In all, he was capped 86 times by England. In November 1934 seven Arsenal players lined up at Highbury for England against Italy. They were Frank Moss, George Male, Eddie Hapgood, Wilf Copping, Ray Bowden, Ted Drake and Cliff Bastin.

EUROPEAN CUP. Arsenal have never won the European Cup but have appeared in the competition on two occasions. They first competed in 1971, reaching the quarter-finals before being knocked out by Ajax. In 1991–92 they reached the second round before losing to Benfica of Portugal 4–2 on aggregate.

EUROPEAN CUP WINNERS CUP. Arsenal have competed in this competition three times. They first appeared during the 1979–80 season and reached the final before losing to Valencia in a penalty shoot-out following a goalless draw in Brussels. In the semi-final they had beaten Juventus. Arsenal next appeared in the European Cup Winners Cup in 1993–94, when they went on to win the trophy, beating Parma 1–0 in the final in Copenhagen. They reached the final with wins over Odense, Standard Liege, Torino and Paris St Germain. They competed again in 1994–95.

EUROPEAN SUPER CUP. Up to the end of the 1993–94 season Arsenal had never appeared in the European Super Cup but their victory in the European Cup Winners Cup of that season was expected to result in a Super Cup game against AC Milan.

Coupe des Vainqueurs de Coupe Européenne 1979/1980.

Europese Beker der Bekerhouders

ARSENAL
&
VALENCIA C.F.

FINALE
14.5.1980 20.15 H/U
Stade du Heysel — Bruxelles
Heizelstadion — Brussel

Programme Officiel:
Officieel Programma: 30 Fr.

EVANS, DENIS. Born in Ellesmere Port, the birthplace of Joe Mercer, Evans made his debut for Arsenal in a friendly in Zurich against Grasshoppers. He was a sturdy defender who even captained the club for a while but was never really a star of the side, never in contention for international honours or recognition of any sort. But he was nevertheless dependable and served Arsenal well, playing more than 200 games in six seasons. He was a one-club man who retired in 1960 through injury but took up a coaching position with the youth side. He is remembered for a bizarre own goal, fortunately scored when Arsenal were leading 4–0. Hearing a whistle, Evans thought the referee had blown for full time and jubilantly slammed the ball from all of 25 yards past his own goalkeeper. Alas, it was not the referee who had blown the whistle but someone in the crowd.

FA CUP. Arsenal first participated in the FA Cup in October 1889, when they beat Lyndhurst 11–0. Arsenal were a non-league side then but went on to the fourth round, where they lost 1–5 to the Swifts.

FA CUP FINALS. Arsenal have appeared in 12 FA Cup finals, winning the trophy on six occasions:
1927 v Cardiff (Wembley) 0–1
1930 v Huddersfield Town (Wembley) 2–0
1932 v Newcastle United (Wembley) 1–2
1936 v Sheffield United (Wembley) 1–0
1950 v Liverpool (Wembley) 2–0
1952 v Newcastle United (Wembley) 0–1
1971 v Liverpool (Wembley) 2–1 *aet*
1972 v Leeds United (Wembley) 0–1
1978 v Ipswich (Wembley) 0–1
1979 v Manchester United (Wembley) 3–2
1980 v West Ham (Wembley) 0–1
1993 v Sheffield Wednesday (Wembley) 1–1 *aet*
   Replay: Arsenal 2 Sheffield Wednesday 1 (Wembley)
Arsenal appeared in three consecutive Cup finals between 1978 and 1980.

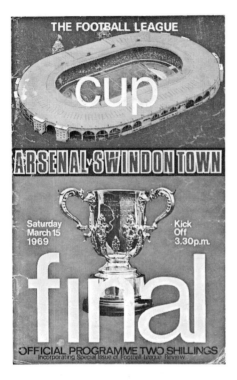

THE FOOTBALL LEAGUE

cup

ARSENAL v SWINDON TOWN

Saturday
March 15
1969

Kick
Off
3.30p.m.

final

OFFICIAL PROGRAMME TWO SHILLINGS
Incorporating Special Issue of Football League Review

CUP FINAL
Arsenal v Manchester United
Football Association Challenge Cup Competition
Saturday 12th May 1979 Kick off 3pm

Wembley

Official Souvenir Programme 50p

ARSENAL v LIVERPOOL
FOOTBALL ASSOCIATION CHALLENGE
CUP COMPETITION

FINAL

SATURDAY 8th MAY 1971
Kick-off 3 p.m.
Official Programme . . . 10p

WEMBLEY Stadium

FOOTBALL ASSOCIATION
CHARITY SHIELD
SATURDAY 11th AUGUST 1979 · KICK-OFF 3.00pm

ARSENAL VERSUS LIVERPOOL
F.A. Challenge Cup Winners 1979   First Division League Champions 1978-79

Wembley 40p Stadium

FA CUP SEMI-FINALS. Arsenal have participated in 18 FA Cup semi-finals up to the end of the 1993–94 season.

FAIRS CUP. This European competition, now known as the UEFA Cup, began its life in 1955. A team representing London were England's first participants, beaten 8–2 on aggregate by Barcelona in the final. Arsenal have taken part in the competition on six occasions. They first participated in 1963–64, reaching the second round. When they next competed, in 1969–70, they reached the final, where they beat Anderlecht 4–3 on aggregate. The following season they again competed and reached the quarter-finals but lost on the away-goal rule to Cologne. The following season the competition changed its name to the UEFA Cup. They then competed for the UEFA Cup in 1978–79, 1981–82 and 1982–83.

FAMILIES. Without any doubt the most famous family to play for Arsenal were the Compton brothers. Leslie was the elder and joined Arsenal in 1931 as an amateur. The following year he turned professional and went on to make more than 300 appearances. His brother Denis also signed initially as an amateur, in September 1932, but did not make his league debut until four years later. He then went on to play 79 games for the club. Both men won wartime England caps, though Leslie was the only one to win a full England cap. Both men were also county cricketers with Middlesex, with Denis, of course, being a well-known England Test cricketer as well.

FANZINES. Like most clubs, Arsenal has its fanzine magazines. Among the most popular are *An Imperfect Match*, *The Gooner*, *One Nil Down Two One Up*, *Up the Arse* and *Highbury Wizard*.

FEWEST WINS IN A SEASON. Arsenal hold the record for the fewest wins in a season in the first division when they managed only three victories in 38 games in 1912–13.

FLOODLIGHTS. Highbury switched on its floodlights for

the first time in 1951 for a friendly match between the Boxers and the Jockeys. But that was part of an experiment. The first important game involving Arsenal to be played under the new lights was on 19 September 1951, when the Gunners played a friendly against Hapoel Tel Aviv of Israel. Arsenal won 6–0 in front of 44,000. Arsenal's floodlights were the first in the country. Lights had actually been fitted before the war to enable evening training and were simply made more powerful for proper competition. Since then the lights have been updated on a number of occasions to comply with Football League and UEFA standards.

FOOTBALL LEAGUE. Arsenal joined the Football League in 1893 and played their first league game, a second division match, on 2 September against Newcastle United. It ended in a 2–2 draw in front of 10,000 at the Manor Ground, Plumstead.

FOOTBALL LEAGUE CUP. Arsenal have twice won the Football League Cup, known at various times as the Milk Cup, the Littlewoods Cup, the Rumbelows Cup and currently the Coca-Cola Cup. Arsenal first participated in the Football League Cup in September 1966, when Gillingham were the visitors to Highbury for a 1–1 draw. The following season Arsenal reached the final only to lose 0–1 to Leeds United at Wembley. The next season they reached the final again, this time going down sensationally 1–3 to Swindon Town, then a third-division side. They did not reach the final again until 1987, when they finally won the trophy with a surprise 2–1 victory over Liverpool. The following season they were there again, but lost for a third time, this time 2–3 against Luton Town. In 1993 they won their second League Cup, beating Sheffield Wednesday 2–1 at Wembley.

Final appearances:

1968 v Leeds United (Wembley) 0–1
1969 v Swindon Town (Wembley) 1–3
1987 v Liverpool (Wembley) 2–1
1988 v Luton Town (Wembley) 2–3
1993 v Sheffield Wednesday (Wembley) 2–1

FOOTBALLER OF THE YEAR. The Football Writers' Footballer of the Year award has been won by Arsenal players on a number of occasions. Past winners have been:
1950 Joe Mercer
1971 Frank McLintock
The Professional Football Association award for Player of the Year has gone to just one Arsenal player:
1979 Liam Brady
The Young Player of the Year award has been won twice by an Arsenal player:
1987 Tony Adams
1989 Paul Merson

FORBES, ALEX. Forbes was already a Scottish international when Arsenal paid Sheffield United £12,500 for his services in February 1948. Before that he was an international ice-hockey player but he converted to football, initially as a centre-forward. He was eventually turned into a wing-half and served Arsenal for nine seasons in that role, playing 300 games. He was a tough, red-haired campaigner who formed an effective partnership with Joe Mercer during his early years. In his first season at Highbury Arsenal won the championship, with Forbes managing 11 games, sadly not enough to qualify him for a championship medal. He made up for it, however, in 1950 with an FA Cup winners medal when the Gunners beat Liverpool at Wembley, with Forbes given the monumental task of looking after fellow Scottish international Billy Liddell. Three years later he did win his championship medal and the following season appeared in the Charity Shield. He left the club at the end of the 1955–56 season following knee trouble and joined Leyton Orient on a free transfer. He later had spells with Fulham and Gravesend before returning to Highbury as a coach in 1962. He won a total of 14 Scottish caps, nine of them while he was an Arsenal player.

FORMER GROUNDS. Since their formation Arsenal have played at the following grounds:
1886–87 Plumstead Common
1887–88 Sportsman Ground

1888–90 Manor Ground
1890–93 Invicta Ground
1893–1913 Manor Ground
1913– Highbury

FORMER NAMES. Arsenal have played under the following names:
1886 Dial Square
1886–91 Royal Arsenal
1891–1914 Woolwich Arsenal

FOTHERINGHAM, JIM. At 6 feet 3 inches, full-back Jim Fotheringham is one of the tallest players ever to pull on an Arsenal shirt. He was a Scot who joined the club as a youngster under Tom Whittaker. He made his league debut at Bolton in November 1954 and although he made a good start his form was not sustained. That was the problem with Fotheringham: he was inconsistent. But he remained with the club for four seasons, playing 76 games, before joining Hearts.

FURNELL, JIM. Born in Clitheroe, Furnell began his playing days with Burnley but with so much goalkeeping talent at Turf Moor he was transferred to Liverpool in February 1962 for £18,000. He immediately took over from Bert Slater in the Liverpool goal but, although he showed early promise as Liverpool clinched the second division title, by November 1962 he had made way for Tommy Lawrence. After that Furnell was always the second-string choice, making only the occasional appearance. He eventually decided to try his luck elsewhere and moved to Arsenal in November 1963 for £15,000, where he made more than 150 appearances. Big and hefty, he was not the most athletic of goalkeepers but he did make up for his inconsistencies with some brave performances. He was replaced by Bob Wilson shortly after the 1968 League Cup final and never won his place back. He left the club six months later, joining Rotherham United for £8,000, and saw his days out at Plymouth Argyle. He was assistant manager at Blackburn Rovers in the early 1980s.

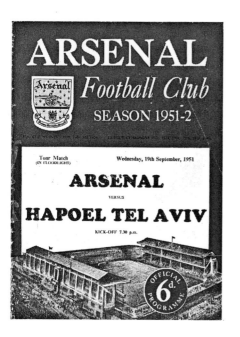

ARSENAL
Football Club
SEASON 1951-2

Tour Match
(IN FLOODLIGHT)

Wednesday, 19th September, 1951

ARSENAL
VERSUS
HAPOEL TEL AVIV

KICK-OFF 7.30 p.m.

OFFICIAL **6ᵈ** PROGRAMME

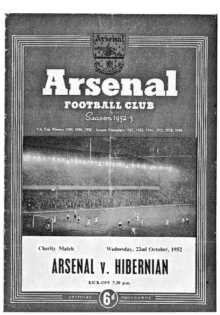

Arsenal
FOOTBALL CLUB
Season 1952-3

F.A. Cup Winners 1930, 1936, 1950. League Champions 1931, 1933, 1934, 1935, 1938, 1948

Charity Match

Wednesday, 22nd October, 1952

ARSENAL v. HIBERNIAN

KICK-OFF 7.30 p.m.

OFFICIAL **6ᵈ** PROGRAMME

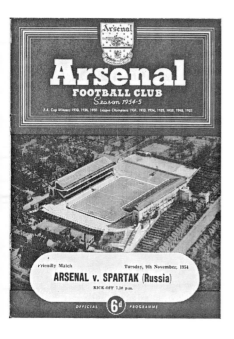

Arsenal
FOOTBALL CLUB
Season 1954-5

F.A. Cup Winners 1930, 1936, 1950. League Champions 1931, 1933, 1934, 1935, 1938, 1948, 1953

Friendly Match

Tuesday, 9th November, 1954

ARSENAL v. SPARTAK (Russia)

KICK-OFF 7.30 p.m.

OFFICIAL **6ᵈ** PROGRAMME

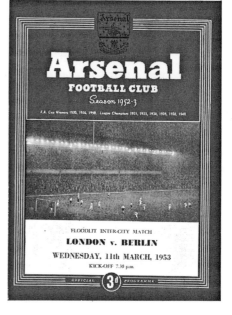

Arsenal
FOOTBALL CLUB
Season 1952-3

F.A. Cup Winners 1930, 1936, 1950. League Champions 1931, 1933, 1934, 1935, 1938, 1948

FLOODLIT INTER-CITY MATCH

LONDON v. BERLIN

WEDNESDAY, 11th MARCH, 1953

KICK-OFF 7.30 p.m.

OFFICIAL **3ᵈ** PROGRAMME

G

GATTING, STEVE. Younger brother of Mike Gatting, the England cricketer. Born in Willesden, it was little wonder that he finished up at Highbury. He was one of many youngsters tried out by Terry Neill and had a good early spell during the 1978–79 season but then lost his place to Brian Talbot. After a few seasons in the reserves he came back to make 23 appearances in the 1980–81 season. He then lost his place again following the signing of Peter Nicholas and left to join Brighton after 65 games. He was a hard-working midfielder rather than a particularly talented one.

GEORGE, CHARLIE. Highbury hero who scored the winning goal in the 1971 Cup final that clinched the Double for Arsenal. Who will ever forget Brian Moore's immortal words: 'It's Charlie George who can hit them'? And, sure enough, he did. Born in Islington, just a stone's throw from Highbury, Charlie came to Arsenal as a youngster, joining the club in May 1966 and turning professional 18 months later. He made his league debut in the first game of the 1969–70 season against Everton and by the end of the season had snatched 15 goals as well as a winners medal in the European Fairs Cup. He was a star from the start and

Charlie George

by the end of the following season would be the darling of Highbury. He was injured early in the 1970–71 season but returned to inspire Arsenal to the Double, hitting 15 goals in all. Tall, slim and with long, straight hair dangling on his shoulders, he was an entertainer, a memorable sight as he burst into penalty areas. He was also precocious, aggressive and a fine taker of any loose chances around goal. After his glorious solo goal in the 1971 final against Liverpool, he played in the losing Cup final of 1972 but from then on was to suffer a series of injuries that would interrupt his Highbury career. In the end he moved to Derby County in 1975 for £90,000 where he proved to be just as popular. Although he was always a favourite with the terraces, he was never quite so popular with his managers, who found him frustrating and annoying, and he never quite matured into the player he had promised to become. He won five England under–23 caps but only one full international cap, and that was while he was with Derby. After Derby he had spells with Southampton, Nottingham Forest, Bournemouth and Brighton. George played almost 200 games for Arsenal, scoring an impressive 70 goals.

GIANTKILLERS. A club of Arsenal's size could never claim the title of ever having been giantkillers but one or two other teams could claim that honour after taking Arsenal's scalp. Perhaps the most embarrassing defeat in the club's history came in January 1933, when Arsenal went to third division Walsall for a third-round FA Cup tie. Arsenal, with players such as David Jack, Alex James and Cliff Bastin, were expected to win comfortably but instead lost 2–0 in what still ranks as one of the biggest Cup upsets of all time. There was also an embrrassment for Arsenal in October 1973 when third division Tranmere Rovers came to Highbury for a League Cup game and won 1–0.

GLASGOW RANGERS. For many seasons before and after the Second World War Arsenal played regular friendly matches against the top Scottish club Glasgow Rangers. Early in the 1933–34 season a crack Arsenal side which had just won the championship lost both home and away to

Rangers. The fixtures continued after the war, often played under floodlights, with Rangers having a good record against the Gunners.

GOALKEEPERS. Over the years the club has boasted some of the finest goalkeepers in the land. Their outstanding stars have included George Swindin, Jack Kelsey, Bob Wilson, Frank Moss, Pat Jennings and, in more recent years, England international David Seaman.

GOALS. The most goals Arsenal have ever scored in one game is 26 against a Parisian XI in December 1904. But that game was only a friendly match. Their highest score in an official match is 12 goals, when they beat Loughborough Town 12–0 in a division-two game in March 1900. The highest number of goals they have scored in the FA Cup is 11. In their first ever FA cup game, in October 1889, they beat Lyndhurst 11–0; they also beat Darwen 11–1 in January 1932. Their highest goal tally in Europe was a 7–0 win over Standard Liege during the 1993/94 season.

GOALS – INDIVIDUAL. Arsenal's Ted Drake is joint holder of the first division record for the highest number of individual goals scored in a game. Against Aston Villa on 14 December 1935 Drake scored all seven goals as Arsenal beat Villa 7–1 at Villa Park.

GOALS – SEASON. The club's highest league goalscorer in any one season remains Ted Drake, who scored 42 league goals as Arsenal won the first division league title in 1934–35.

GOALSCORERS – LEAGUE. Arsenal's top league goalscorer is Cliff Bastin, who struck 150 league goals during his years at Highbury. But only eight players have hit more than 100 league goals for the club.
1. Cliff Bastin 150
2. Jimmy Brain 125
3. Doug Lishman 125
4. Ted Drake 124

5. David Jack 113
6. John Radford 111
7. Joe Hulme 107
8. Reg Lewis 103
9. Jack Lambert 98
10. David Herd 97

GOALSCORER–OVERALL. More than a dozen players have hit a century of goals for Arsenal in all competitions. The club's top marksman is Cliff Bastin, with 196 goals. The Century Club:
Cliff Basin 196
John Radford 188
Doug Lishman 173
Jimmy Brain 159
Reg Lewis 158
Ted Drake 150
David Herd 143
Joe Hulme 138
Don Roper 134
Jack Lambert 133
David Jack 130
Cliff Holton 125
Frank Stapleton 125
John Coleman 110
Alan Sunderland 101

GOOING, BILL. Centre-forward of the early years of the twentieth century. Yorkshire-born Gooing began his career with Sheffield Wednesday but failed to make much impression and moved on to Chesterfield in 1899. Two years later Arsenal signed him. He went straight into the Gunners first team and at the end of his first season they were fourth in the table. Gooing scored 15 goals that season and 20 the following season as Arsenal improved slightly, just missing out on promotion. But the following season, 1903–4, he played a major role, scoring 21 goals as Arsenal wound up in second spot to win promotion. But life in the first division was not quite so easy. The goals were more difficult to come by – just three in 14 games – and Gooing lost his place to Andy Ducat. A year later he joined Northampton Town. He had made 129 appearances for the Gunners, scoring 59 goals.

GORING, PETER. During the post-war years Peter Goring was a fine sight in an Arsenal shirt. Slim, enterprising and a brave runner with the ball, he went on to make almost 300 appearances for Arsenal, scoring 67 goals. A former butcher's boy, he joined the club in January 1948 from Cheltenham Town. He made his first appearance as Arsenal toured Brazil in May 1949 and a few months later made his league debut as the new season kicked off. By the end of that season Goring had scored 29 goals, 21 of those in the league, and had also played a major part as Arsenal went on to win the FA Cup, giving a fine performance at Wembley in Arsenal's 2–0 win over Liverpool. In 1953 he picked up a league championship medal but by then the goals were beginning to dry up. After that season he would score only two more goals for the Gunners. Injuries were also taking their toll but, in an inspired move, manager Tom Whittaker switched him to wing-half and brought about a new lease of life. In 1956 he was appointed team captain, a role in which he revelled. His career had fallen into two distinct parts: the early goalscoring years and the later, mature years as a strong wing-half. At the end of the 1959–60 season he was given a free transfer and played for Boston United and Romford before quitting the game to return to Cheltenham and the greengrocery business. Goring was never capped but he was a member of the FA team that toured the West Indies in 1955.

GOULD, BOBBY. Came to Arsenal from Coventry in February 1968 for £90,000. He made a promising start and although he went on to score 23 goals in 72 appearances he was never a particularly impressive striker. When the likes of Ray Kennedy and John Radford began to emerge, Gould found himself pushed out of the side and in June 1970 he opted for a move to Wolves. He then played for a host of clubs, including a couple of spells with Wolves.

He later became a successful manager, particularly with Coventry and Wimbledon.

GRAHAM, ALEX. Scotsman who played for Arsenal during the first part of the century. He joined the club from Larkhall United in December 1911, making his debut the following year in a close-season friendly on the continent. But his performance did not impress enough to warrant a league spot and Graham was forced to wait until Christmas Day 1925 before he pulled on an Arsenal shirt in a league game. But with an abundance of talent up front, Graham could not secure a regular place. He made just a dozen league appearances in his first season and 13 the following season. Then in the 1914–15 season he finally established himself, though by then he had been converted into a halfback. War then intervened to further disrupt his career but he was not forgotten and after the war continued in Arsenal's half-back line for another five seasons. But it was something of a blank period for Arsenal and Graham won no honours with the club other than a London FA Challenge Cup winners medal. He was capped just once by Scotland, playing against Ireland in Belfast in February 1921. In all, he played 204 games for the Gunners, scoring 25 goals. In December 1924 he was transferred to Brentford, later becoming assistant manager.

GRAHAM, GEORGE. Player and manager. It is little wonder that a bronze bust of George Graham has been placed in the foyer at Highbury alongside that of Herbert Chapman. Graham, without any doubt, deserves to be considered among the greatest servants Arsenal have ever known. He was one of Bertie Mee's first signings when he arrived from Chelsea in September 1966. Although he came from Scotland, Graham's footballing days had begun with Aston Villa in 1961. He met with little success at Villa Park and after just eight appearances he signed for Chelsea during the 1964 close season. At Stamford Bridge he began to show real promise, enough to persuade Mee to bring him to Highbury. He was an instant success, scoring 21 goals in his second season even though he was never a

George Graham

genuine goalscorer. After that he dropped back into his more natural position in the midfield and was soon on the medal trail. He claimed a European Fairs Cup medal in 1970 and then the following season was picking up league and Cup medals. He was a general in the Gunners midfield, creating chances, working furiously to win the ball and racing with equal effect back into defence. Then, surprisingly, 18 months after winning the Double he was sold to Manchester United for £120,000. He later had spells with Portsmouth and Crystal Palace, helping Palace to promotion before retiring to take up a coaching job with them. He then coached at Queens Park Rangers and was appointed manager of Millwall in December 1982. Millwall were on the brink of relegation to the fourth division but Graham saved them and even took them into the second division in 1985 before Arsenal appointed him as manager in May 1986. In his first season in charge at Highbury Arsenal finished in sixth spot and won the Littlewoods Cup. It was an impressive start. Then came the highlights: a league championship in 1989 and a second one two years later. In 1993 Arsenal lifted the FA Cup and the League Cup, followed a season later by the European Cup Winners Cup. Graham had blended a fine young side together, many of his players home grown. There were admittedly expensive recruits in players like Seaman, Linighan and Wright but the bulk of his team had cost little. Graham has always built for the future, never resting on his laurels but continually adding to the squad and has fashioned a side that looks set for many more honours.

GRAY, ARCHIE. One of the first great Scottish players to wear the Arsenal colours. Gray was born in Govan in Glasgow in 1883 but although he played junior and amateur football in Glasgow he found himself joining the Edinburgh side Hibernian. In 1902 he won a Scottish Cup winners medal as Hibernian beat Celtic in the final. A year later he was capped by his country, appearing for Scotland against Ireland and also representing the Scottish League against the Irish League. In May 1904 he left Hibernian to join Woolwich Arsenal, immediately winning his first-team place and becoming a regular over the next seven seasons. In all, he played 233 games for the Gunners but failed to score one goal. That was hardly surprising considering he was a full-back who rarely ventured beyond the halfway line. In April 1912 he moved to Fulham and eventually returned to Glasgow.

GRIFFITHS, ARFON. Signed from Wrexham in January 1961 for £14,000, Griffiths was heralded as the new George Eastham. Arsenal had beaten off some big rivals to sign Griffiths but he turned out to be a disaster. He looked totally out of his depth in the first division and after just 15 games and a couple of goals he was on his way back to Wrexham for £4,000 less. He was far more at home in North Wales and went on to enjoy a distinguished career with the Welsh club as player and later as manager.

GROVES, PERRY. Nephew of former Arsenal favourite Vic Groves. Groves, with his sharp ginger hair, cuts an unmistakable figure in an Arsenal shirt and has earned him the nickname 'Tintin'. His pacey, sometimes even erratic, runs have resulted in many a goal for the Gunners. None will be better remembered than his race down the flanks in the Littlewoods Cup final against Liverpool after he had come on as a substitute, to cross for Charlie Nicholas to hit the winning goal. He was manager George Graham's first signing when he bought the youngster from Colchester United for £75,000 in September 1986. Groves took time to establish himself but went on to win league championship medals in 1989 and 1991.

GROVES, VIC. Popular player of the mid–1950s and early 1960s. Born in London, Groves was an amateur international with Leytonstone and Walthamstow Avenue before he joined Tottenham Hotspur. But he made just four league appearances for the Spurs and was allowed to move on to Leyton Orient, even though he had scored three goals for them. It was at Brisbane Road that he really began to make his name, adding an England B cap to his schoolboy and youth honours. He joined Arsenal in November 1955 in a £30,000 deal that also brought Stan Charlton to Highbury. He scored on his debut against Sheffield United but a promising career was soon interrupted by injuries. Nothing seemed to go right for him. He was in and out of the team for one reason or another and it was not until 1959 that he really settled. The inspiration was not only to make him captain but to drop him back into the midfield where he was less susceptible to injury. Groves took on a new maturity and began to show the potential that had always been there. In one remarkable game against Everton in September 1958 at Goodison Park Groves scored and then hit the woodwork three times. It hardly mattered as Arsenal won 6–1 but had Groves's goals gone in then surely a few new records would have been created. He picked up an England under–23 cap but won no other honours as a Gunner other than a few minor local cup medals. But Groves was always a joy to watch; a fine passer of the ball and a robust tackler. In 1964, with new boss Billy Wright looking to rebuild the side, Groves moved on, joining Canterbury City. But within a year he had retired from the game. His nephew is Perry Groves, another Gunners favourite. Vic Groves played 271 games, scoring 58 goals.

GUEST PLAYERS. During the Second World War league clubs were allowed to field guest players from local barracks as it was often difficult to obtain leave every week for their own players, who might be barracked many miles away. Among those who guested for Arsenal were Stan Mortensen, Bill Shankly, Andy Beattie, Stanley Matthews, and Len Goulden.

GUNNERS. Nickname of Arsenal, given because of the club's original links with the Woolwich Arsenal munitions factory.

H

HAPGOOD, EDDIE. One of the outstanding names in Arsenal's long history. Hapgood came to Highbury in October 1927, signed by Herbert Chapman for just £1,000 from Kettering. He made his league debut almost immediately but did not hold down a regular place until a season or so later. But once he was in the team he became almost an ever-present over the next ten years and went on to become one of Arsenal's finest ever full-backs. He won his first England cap in May 1933 against Italy and went on to win a total of 30 caps. He was also captain of England on 21 occasions, winning more caps than any other England player during the inter-war years. He continued playing first-team football for Arsenal until war broke out and although he remained on Arsenal's books during the war he later went off to manage Blackburn Rovers and Watford. He also played 13 wartime internationals for England, again captaining them on many occasions. His honours were impressive: five championship medals, two FA Cup winners medals, one runners-up medal and appearances in six Charity Shield matches. With George Male alongside him, Arsenal had one of the strongest defences in their history. Two committed, elegant defenders, determined to play themselves out of trouble rather than kick the ball upfield. Hapgood played a total of 487 games for the Gunners.

HAT TRICK – CHAMPIONSHIPS. Between 1933 and 1936 Arsenal won three successive league titles to become only the second club to achieve such a feat.

HAT TRICK HEROES. Arsenal's hat trick hero has to be Ted Drake, who during the club's championship season of 1934–35 hit seven hat tricks. He struck 42 league goals that season, including eight goals in consecutive games. The following season Drake hit seven against Aston Villa to set a new first division record. Another hat trick hero was Doug Lishman, who during the 1951–52 season hit three consecutive hat tricks in the league at Highbury. His first came on 27 October 1951 as Arsenal beat Fulham 4–3. His second arrived on 10 November as they thrashed West Brom 6–3 and then on 24 November Lishman scored his third successive hat trick at Highbury as the Gunners beat Bolton 4–2.

HAVERTY, JOE. Republic of Ireland international of the 1950s. Haverty joined the Gunners from St Patrick's Athletic in Dublin and made his debut at Goodison Park on the same day as Jimmy Bloomfield. But it would be another two years before he became a regular at Highbury. He then went on to make 165 appearances before he left the club to join Blackburn Rovers in the summer of 1961. At 5 feet 3 inches Haverty was one of the smallest men ever to play for Arsenal but what he lacked in size he made up for in spirit. Someone even dubbed him the 'laughing leprechaun'. Haverty was a tricky little winger, though he was never too fond of mixing it with towering defenders. But he had a strong, accurate shot and netted 35 goals for Arsenal during his days. He won his first international cap in 1956 against Holland and went on to win 15 caps while he was at Highbury. He played his final game for the Republic in 1967, his 32nd international. After Blackburn, Haverty had spells with Millwall, Celtic, Bristol Rovers and Shelbourne.

HAWLEY, JOHN. Another striker signed to fill the void left by Frank Stapleton. Hawley came from Sunderland but was well known to Arsenal manager Terry Neill when the two had been at Hull City together. Neill paid £50,000 for Hawley, who had a useful goalscoring record. But in the top division the goals failed to materialise, only three in 15 outings. When Tony Woodcock arrived in the summer of 1982 it heralded the end of Hawley's Highbury days. A year later he went to Hong Kong on a free transfer.

HAYES, MARTIN. Another youngster who came up through the ranks of junior football at Highbury. Hayes made his debut in November 1985 against Oxford United, replacing Graham Rix. He began well but a short time later was offered the chance to join Huddersfield Town. He turned the opportunity down and although it seemed that he was not really wanted at Highbury he was lucky enough to get a few more first-team opportunities. Eventually, he made the break into regular first-team football during the 1986–87 season. He was a revelation and went on to net 24 league and Cup goals and ended the season with a Littlewoods Cup winners medal. His pacey running left defenders bewildered and he looked to be heading for an outstanding career. But like so many promising forwards, the following season he was not half as impressive. His form continued to decline, although he did come off the bench enough times to pick up a league championship medal in 1989. But somehow the fire and pace had disappeared. In the summer of 1990 he was sold to Glasgow Celtic for £650,000. Hayes played a total of 92 games for Arsenal, scoring 34 goals.

HEANEY, NEIL. Although he was born in Middlesbrough Heaney came through the junior ranks of Highbury. He first played in the Football League while on loan to Hartlepool during the 1990–91 season. He also had a successful loan period with Cambridge United from January to March 1992, scoring on his debut. He returned to Highbury and made his Arsenal debut as a substitute away to Sheffield United in April 1992. Heaney was a regular England youth-team player and graduated to the England under-21 side in 1992.

HENDERSON, JACKIE. Joined Arsenal from Wolverhampton Wanderers for £20,000 in the autumn of 1958. Prior to Wolves, Henderson had played with Portsmouth. A Scot, he had won the first of his seven international caps in 1953 while he was with Portsmouth and although he would enjoy a short return to international soccer he would win only two caps while he was with Arsenal. He began well at Highbury, netting 12 times in his 21 league appearances that season as Arsenal finished in third spot. But that was to prove the peak of his Highbury career. A versatile attacker, he preferred to play on the wing and remained at Arsenal until January 1962 when he joined Fulham. He played 111 games for Arsenal, scoring 29 goals.

HERD, DAVID. It was always surprising that David Herd did not sign for either of the Manchester clubs when he was young, given that his father, Alex Herd, had been an outstanding City player. Instead, young David joined Stockport County, where he played alongside his father. As it was, David made it to the top with a transfer to Arsenal in August 1954 for £10,000 and went on to play 228 games, scoring 143 goals. A tall, powerful striker, Herd also won international honours. For three seasons he topped the goalscoring charts at Highbury but never seemed to figure in Arsenal's long-term plans. On numerous occasions they tried to unload him, offering him to Huddersfield in part-exchange for Denis Law and to Newcastle for George Eastham. Eventually he went to Manchester United in the summer of 1961 for £35,000 and went on to give United outstanding service, winning league championship and FA Cup winners medals. United's gain was undoubtedly Arsenal's loss. Herd won a total of five Scottish caps, all while he was at Highbury. He later played with Stoke City and then became manager of Lincoln.

HIGHBURY. Arsenal's home ground since 1913. The club moved there from Manor Road at the end of the 1912–13 season, a season that saw the Gunners relegated. Neither Tottenham nor Clapton Orient wanted Arsenal, however, fearing that a third club in north London might be one too many. Islington Borough Council did not want them either, claiming that the stadium would decrease property values. The new ground was situated on the playing fields of St John's College of Divinity and cost the club £20,000 for a 21-year lease. The stadium was designed by Archibald Leitch, the most famous of all football stadium architects. It was opened on 6 September 1913 but was only half completed, resembling a builder's yard more than a football ground. Because it was such a large ground, Highbury soon became a focal point, staging its first international in March 1920. But it was not until Herbert Chapman arrived that the real Highbury began to take shape. The ground was formally purchased for £64,000 when the lease came up for renewal and major redevelopment began in 1931. A new west stand was built, designed by Claude Waterlow Ferrier, and was opened in December 1932 by HRH the Prince of Wales, later to be King Edward VIII. The cost was £50,000 with seats for 4,000 and standing room for 17,000. Chapman also erected a clock on the North Bank, much to the annoyance of the Football Association. In 1935 the North Bank was covered and the clock moved to the opposite terracing, which then became known as the Clock End. A year later work began on building a new East Stand to house all the administrative offices. It seated 4,000 spectators on the top tier, 4,000 in the lower tier with a paddock for standing below and was formally opened in October 1936. It was without doubt the finest Football League ground in the country. For the next 50 years there was little further development at Highbury. Floodlights were added in 1951 and switched on for a friendly against Hapoel Tel Aviv of Israel. Undersoil heating was installed in 1964. During the Second World War Highbury was closed for football and used as a major first-aid post and air-raid patrol centre. During the air raids on London a 1,000-lb bomb fell on the training pitch while other bombs destroyed the North Bank roof. It was not until the introduction of the Taylor proposals in the early 1990s, following the

Hillsborough disaster, that any further changes took place. Since then both the Clock End and the North Bank have been seated in a major redevelopment. Executive boxes have also been added in a tasteful construction that has maintained the spirit of the ground's previous architects. Highbury, which can now seat 39,000 in considerable comfort, is today one of the finest grounds in the country.

HILL, COLIN. Made his Arsenal debut against Norwich in April 1983 as partner to David O'Leary but proved to be ineffective. He was later pushed into the right-back spot and went on to play just over 50 games for the club. But the arrival of Viv Anderson ended his days in that role. A short time later he was transferred to the Portuguese club Maritimo. Later he returned to England, playing with Colchester United and then Sheffield United, where he won Northern Ireland international honours.

HILLIER, DAVID. One of the unluckiest players around Highbury. After helping to beat Spurs in the FA Cup semifinal in 1993, he was injured two days later and missed both Wembley appearances against Sheffield Wednesday. He skippered the 1988 Arsenal FA Youth Cup winning side and is already an England under-21 international. He began as an associated schoolboy in January 1984. He made his league debut in September 1990 against Leeds United. Hillier also missed Arsenal's European Cup Winners Cup final in 1994 due to injury. A good tackler but a limited passer of the ball, Arsenal have high hopes of him.

HOLLINS, JOHN. Hollins may have come to Highbury late in the day – he was 33 years old when he signed in July 1979 – but still managed to give five years devoted service to the club. Prior to joining Arsenal, he played with Chelsea and Queens Park Rangers, with both clubs cashing in on a man who they assumed was past his best. But rather than go into decline Hollins seemed to get better with the years. At the age of 36 he became captain and helped Arsenal reach two semi-finals. He was an inspiring example to everyone at the club, enthusiastic, committed, combative and at £75,000 had to be one of the best pieces of business the club had done in years. He remained with Arsenal until the summer of 1983, when Chelsea tempted him back to Stamford Bridge with the offer of a job as player-coach. He later became manager of Chelsea. Hollins played 164 games for Arsenal, scoring 13 goals.

HOLTON, CLIFF. Signed by Arsenal shortly after the war in November 1947 from Oxford City. He was initially a defender but three years later the Arsenal manager tried him at centre-forward and sparked off a highly successful career with the Gunners. He made his debut in December 1950 against Stoke City and went on to play more than 250 games for the club, scoring 125 goals. It was an impressive scoring rate and helped Arsenal to the league championship in 1953 when he scored 19 league goals. Later in his career he switched to wing-half and was also captain of the side. His first ever Cup tie was the 1952 Cup final against Newcastle but his goalscoring touch deserted him that day as Newcastle won the Cup. In October 1958 he signed for Watford and later had spells with Northampton Town, Crystal Palace, Charlton Athletic and Orient, where he added a total of 210 more goals to his career total, which must have made Arsenal wonder if perhaps they had sold him too early or should at least have retained him as a striker. A knee injury finally brought an end to his career in 1969.

HOME RECORD. Arsenal's best home record was for the 1970–71 season, when they were unbeaten in 21 games. Eighteen of these were won and three drawn.

HORNSBY, BRIAN. Former England schoolboy and youth international striker who had few opportunities at Highbury, with John Radford, Ray Kennedy, Charlie George and Brian Kidd around during his time. He managed just 23 games, scoring six goals, before joining Shrewsbury Town for £20,000 in June 1976. He later had his best days with Sheffield Wednesday.

HOWARD, PAT. Joined Arsenal from Newcastle for £50,000 in September 1976. A central defender, he was bought as a replacement for Terry Mancini but he never really looked the part and within the year he was sold to Birmingham City for £40,000. By then Willie Young had been signed and there was no room for Howard. He had played just 19 games.

HOWE, DON. Player, coach and manager. Howe had a particularly mixed career as an Arsenal player. He came to the club in April 1964, a £35,000 signing from West Bromwich Albion by Billy Wright. Howe was already an established English international with 23 caps to his name. Many thought that perhaps he was already past his peak when he signed for the Gunners but after a nervous start he began to show his class. Unfortunately, he then broke his leg and was faced with a long lay off. He returned but by then had lost pace and confidence. He played just one more game for the club before retiring. He remained at Highbury, however, to take up a coaching post under Bertie Mee. Between them they went on to lift the Fairs Cup and then the Double. Howe then left Highbury to take over as manager at his old club, West Brom. That was followed by spells as a coach with the Turkish club Galatasary and Leeds United before he returned to Highbury as chief coach in 1977. Howe again formed an effective partnership with his manager, this time Terry Neill, taking the club to three FA Cup finals as well as the European Cup Winners Cup final. When Terry Neill left the club in 1983 Howe moved up, initially as caretaker manager, but was confirmed in the job the following April. Under Howe Arsenal began to improve, regularly finishing in the top ten but there were no honours – and at Highbury that meant disappointment. In March 1986, as the pressure grew for his resignation, he quit the club. Since then he has coached at various clubs, including Wimbledon, and enjoyed a spell under Bobby Robson as coach to the England side. Howe has always been regarded as one of the top coaches in the business, a man, however, who tends to put an emphasis on defence, rather than attack. Perhaps this was not surprising given

Don Howe

his long and distinguished career as a full-back.

HUDSON, ALAN. When Alan Hudson signed for Arsenal in December 1967 fans were ecstatic at the prospect. Hudson had cost the Gunners £200,000 from Stoke City but even though it was a massive fee, Arsenal were just one of many clubs eager to get the young man's signature. But there were doubters. Hudson had begun his career with Chelsea, bursting on to the scene with some dynamic performances. He undoubtedly had an abundance of talent but he also seemed to have an attitude problem. Chelsea had let him go to Stoke, where he seemed to settle and mature, even winning England honours. When he performed he was sensational but all too often he drifted out of games, looking disinterested. At Highbury he was paired in the midfield with Liam Brady – it should have been one of the most productive pairings in English football but, unfortunately it was not. Hudson was back to his Chelsea days. He played in the 1978 FA Cup final but gave a far from convincing performance and five months later was sold to

Seattle Sounders for £95,000. In all he had played just 46 games for the club and had not even scored one goal.

HULME, JOE. One of Herbert Chapman's first signings. Hulme joined Arsenal for £3,500 from Blackburn Rovers in early 1926. Prior to that, he had played with York City. At Blackburn he made 73 appearances, scoring just four goals in two years. But Chapman spotted the potential and over the next 13 seasons Hulme would play just over 400 games for the Gunners, netting 138 goals. He was reckoned to be one of the fastest and most slippery wingers in the game but also had a deadly accurate cross, as well as a powerful shot. He won his first England cap against Scotland in April 1927 and his ninth and final cap six years later, also against Scotland. During his time at Highbury he helped Arsenal to three league championships and played in four FA Cup finals. Then, in 1938, he joined Huddersfield Town and made another trip to Wembley, only to be on the losing side for the third time. Like so many Arsenal players, Hulme also played first-class cricket with Middlesex. He ended his playing days with Huddersfield and after the war became manager of Tottenham Hotspur until 1949 when he took up journalism.

HUNDRED GOALS. Arsenal have scored more than 100 league goals in a season on a number of occasions, with their best performance in the 1930–31 season when they struck 127 goals.

I

INTER-LEAGUE MATCHES. Arsenal have hosted a number of inter-league matches. The first time they hosted such a game was in November 1901 at the Manor Ground, Plumstead. That day the Football League beat the Irish League 9–0 in front of 12,000 spectators. The next time was in October 1914 when the Football League beat the Southern League 2–1, this time at Highbury. In March 1921 Highbury was again the venue as the Football League beat the Scottish League 1–0. Highbury then had to wait until March 1960 for the next contest as the Football League again beat the Scottish League 1–0. In November 1962 the Football League beat the Italian League 3–2, the last time Highbury was used for such a game.

INTERNATIONAL CAPS – FIRST. The first Arsenal player ever to win an international honour was Caesar Jenkyns, who was capped for Wales against Scotland in 1896.

INTERNATIONAL CAPS – MOST. Arsenal's most capped player is Kenny Sansom, who made 77 appearances for England while he was at the club. He went on to make a total of 86 appearances for his country.

INTERNATIONAL MATCHES. Highbury has been the venue of many England international matches, its first in March 1920 when England lost 1–2 to Wales. There was better luck for England three years later, however, when they beat Belgium 6–1 at Highbury. In December 1931 there was another fine result for England as they defeated Spain 7–1. One of the most memorable matches, however, was the 3–2 defeat of the reigning world champions Italy in November 1934, when seven Arsenal players lined up for England. Two years later England beat Hungary 6–2 and then in 1938 they beat a FIFA side 3–0. After the war Highbury became a regular home for England, with games against France and Sweden in 1947, against Switzerland in 1948, against Yugoslavia in 1950, and against France in 1951. Highbury then had to wait until 1961 to see England again, as they beat Luxembourg 4–1.

INVICTA GROUND. Arsenal's home ground between 1890 and 1893.

ITALY. On 14 November 1934 seven Arsenal players lined up in England shirts to face Italy at Highbury. At the time Italy were the world champions, having just won the World Cup but they were to be beaten 3–2. The seven Arsenal players on duty that day were Frank Moss in goal, George Male and Eddie Hapgood in defence, Wilf Copping at wing-half; and Ray Bowden, Ted Drake and Cliff Bastin in attack. The England trainer that day was also an Arsenal man – Tom Whittaker – while the radio commentator was George Allison, the secretary-manager of the Gunners. Ted Drake scored one of the goals with Eric Brook of Manchester City hitting the other two.

J

JACK, DAVID. The first footballer to break the £10,000 transfer barrier. David Bone Nightingale Jack was signed by Herbert Chapman in October 1928 when Chapman paid Bolton Wanderers £10,980 for his services. It was a staggering sum of money but Chapman knew what he was doing and in time David Jack would go on to repay his huge transfer fee many times over. Although he had been born in Bolton, Jack began his football career with Plymouth Argyle, where his father was manager. It was not until 1921 that he returned to his birthplace, joining Bolton Wanderers for £3,000. With Bolton Jack went on to win two FA Cup winners medals, scoring the first ever goal at Wembley and picking up four England caps. He won his first cap in 1924, playing against Wales, and won a second cap later that year against Scotland. He then had to wait four years before he was recalled. He was a prolific goalscorer, hitting 143 goals in 295 appearances for Bolton. And it was that kind of strike rate that impressed Chapman. Arsenal were in need of a star. Charlie Buchan was set to retire and somehow had to be replaced. Jack was the obvious man and even though it did mean a hefty fee Chapman had no hesitations. At Highbury Jack was even more successful, winning three championship medals and a third FA

David Jack

Cup winners medal to make him one of the most honoured footballers of the time. He also picked up a losers medal in the 1932 Cup final and added a further five caps to his name, though again there were unusually large gaps between selections. But, as compensation, Jack did become the England captain, the first Arsenal player ever to achieve the distinction. He also made five appearances for the Football League. Jack was an inside forward, whose best position was at inside-right. He liked to have a shot at goal but was equally adept at carrying the ball into the area. He scored 130 goals for the Gunners in 223 appearances, an even better strike rate than in his younger days at Bolton. During the 1930–31 season he struck 31 league goals in 35 outings. He left Arsenal during the summer of 1934 to become manager of Southend United and later held a similar position with Middlesbrough.

JACKSON, JIMMY. Born in Cambuslang in Scotland, Jackson's family emigrated to Australia when he was only two years old. In Australia Jackson became obsessed with football, showing remarkable talent. He decided on a career in the game and returned to Scotland, eventually joining Glasgow Rangers. He later had a spell with Newcastle United and then found his way to Woolwich Arsenal in May 1899. He made his debut for the club in the opening game of the following season and went on to play 268 games, captaining the club as they won promotion to the first division. Jackson was a left-back, a strong defender and an outstanding captain. At the end of the 1904–5 season he left the club to become player-manager of Leyton and then joined West Ham, where he made a further 25 league appearances. He eventually returned to Scotland, re-joining Glasgow Rangers.

JAMES, ALEX. Few names in the history of Arsenal Football Club are more famous than that of Alex James. Along with Everton's Dixie Dean, he was undoubtedly one of the two most famous names in inter-war football. James was born in Lanarkshire in 1901 and began playing with Raith Rovers in 1922. Three years later he was transferred to

Preston North End, where he scored 53 goals in 147 games before signing for Arsenal in June 1929 for £8,750, a huge fee in those days. By then James was well on his way to creating his massive reputation. He had been capped by his country, winning his first cap in 1926 against Wales. Two years later he was a member of the famous Scotland side that ran England dizzy at Wembley to win 5–1. James was the original midfielder, an inside-forward who could alternate with the role of wing-half. In 1930 he won an FA Cup winners medal as Arsenal beat Huddersfield 2–0, scoring Arsenal's second goal himself. Then in 1936 he picked up a second winners medal. As well as that, James won four league championship medals with the Gunners and brought his total of Scottish caps to eight, surprisingly few considering his impact on the game. By the end of his playing days he was probably the most honoured footballer of all, and indeed had he remained at Highbury another season he would doubtless have picked up a fifth championship medal. Manager Herbert Chapman built his great side of the 1930s around James, looking to him as the man who could inspire and control the game. Few in the game's history have ever been able to do it as effectively as James. He retired in 1937 after making 275 appearances for the Gunners and scoring 29 goals, and went into journalism. But a short time after the war he returned to Highbury to help coach the club's junior sides.

JENKINS, DAVID. Progressed through the ranks at Highbury, making his debut during the 1966–67 season. He initially attracted much talk but he never lived up to his promise. He played in the 1968 League Cup final when Arsenal were beaten by Leeds United and scored a memorable hat trick against Scunthorpe in the League Cup, but by then there was increasing competition for places and in October 1968 he joined Tottenham. He was equally ineffective there and after a couple of years moved on to Brentford, followed by spells with Hereford, Newport, Shrewsbury and Workington.

JENKYNS, CAESAR. Probably better known for his years

as a Manchester United player. Jenkyns has the distinction of being Arsenal's first ever international. Born in Wales, Jenkyns played his early football in the Midlands with Small Heath, later to become Birmingham City. He won four international caps with them and was transferred to Woolwich Arsenal in April 1895. He played for just one season, a tall, majestic centre-half, appearing in 53 games and scoring nine goals. He captained the side for most of that season and in 1896 became the club's first international when he played for Wales against Scotland. He then moved to Newton Heath, later known as Manchester United, where he enjoyed a distinguished career.

JENNINGS, PAT. One of the finest goalkeepers ever to play for the Gunners. It came as something of a surprise when Tottenham agreed to let Jennings come to Highbury. He may have been 32 years old but he was nowhere near the end of his career. And to prove Spurs wrong Jennings went on to give eight seasons' service to Arsenal before leaving at the end of the 1984–85 season. By then he had played a staggering 378 games for the Gunners. Tottenham then made up for their earlier mistake by re-signing the genial Irishman for a second spell. When his career ended he had played more than 1,000 games in English football. He had also won a record 119 caps for Northern Ireland. Jennings began his goalkeeping with Watford in May 1963. Twelve months later he joined Tottenham for £27,000 and went on to give remarkable service over the next 13 years. In that time he won a UEFA Cup winners medal, an FA Cup winners medal, two runners-up medals, two League Cup winners medals and was Footballer of the Year. Then, much to everyone's astonishment, Tottenham, convinced that he was near the end of his career, let him go. But Tottenham's loss was Arsenal's gain as Jennings continued to give unstinting service to his new club. Jennings was without doubt one of the finest goalkeepers of all time. He was as safe as any keeper has ever been and was never one to go leaping unnecessarily about his goalmouth. His strength was in his positional play, though he was equally capable of a reflex save or an acrobatic leap. Jennings won his first cap for Northern Ireland in 1964 while he was with Watford and picked up his final cap 22 years later. By then he had returned to Tottenham and had even had a spell on loan to Everton. At Arsenal he won an FA Cup winners medal, two runners-up medals, a European Cup Winners Cup runners-up medal and 42 caps.

JENSEN, JOHN. After playing a splendid role in Denmark's European Championship winning side in 1992 Arsenal paid Brondby £1.1 million for his services. Jensen is a tall and effective central defender with a fine ability to read the game. He took a little time to adjust to the English game but since then he has gone on to give sterling service for the Gunners. He won an FA Cup winners medal in 1993, appearing in both games in the final, but missed out on Arsenal's victory in the Coca-Cola Cup final. He also missed the 1994 European Cup Winners Cup final through injury. Not known for his goalscoring, Jensen remains highly popular with the Highbury fans.

JOHN, BOB. Welshman Bob John set a new club record during the 1930s when he made 421 league appearances for the Gunners and a total of 521 appearances. It was a record that was to stand for 37 years until George Armstrong eventually overhauled his total. John originally played with Barry Town and Caerphilly and was fully expected to sign for Cardiff City but Arsenal nipped in and in January 1922 he arrived at Highbury. A year later he was a regular first-team player and continued to turn out until just prior to the Second World War. His league appearances, however, were fairly infrequent after 1935. Half-back John was a regular member of Arsenal's first championship side and also played in the sides that won three successive titles, winning medals for the first two championships. But he did not qualify for a medal with the side that won the third successive title. John also won an FA Cup winners medal as well as two losers medals. He won his first Welsh cap in 1923 and his final, and 15th Cap, 13 years later.

JOHNSTON, GEORGE. Bertie Mee's rebuilding programme might in the end have brought the league and Cup to Highbury but *en route* Mee also brought a few players to the club who could best be described as misfits. George Johnston figured among them. He came from Cardiff in a £25,000 deal but he was yet another striker and the club would soon discover that it had one too many. Johnston made just 20 appearances, scored five goals and then went to Birmingham City, where he fared no better.

JONES, BRYN. A record signing by Arsenal when they paid Wolverhampton Wanderers £14,000 for his services in 1938. Jones was signed at a time when Arsenal's fortunes were still at a height, though in fact the side was ageing and would never be the same again. The team that had achieved so much during the 1930s was on the wane after he joined and in particular Alex James had never been replaced. Jones was signed as his replacement but had barely had the chance to pull on an Arsenal shirt before war broke out. He played just 30 games before the war and although Arsenal might well have matured into a fine new side they never had the opportunity. By the time the war was over Jones was getting old himself and his best years were behind him. After that it was downhill all the way for him. Arsenal went on to lift the championship in 1948 but Jones only played seven games and was no longer part of the club's long-term plans. He played just 92 games for the Gunners, even though he spent 11 years with them. He finally left the club in June 1949 to become player-coach of Norwich City. He won his first international cap in 1935 and went on to make 17 appearances for Wales, winning seven of those caps while he was an Arsenal man. Jones was an attacking inside-forward but in a side that found scoring goals difficult, Jones ended up with just nine, a disappointing reflection on all his endeavours over the years.

JONES, CHARLIE. A member of Herbert Chapman's outstanding side of the 1930s. Born in South Wales, Charlie Jones kicked off his career with Cardiff City but injury and loss of form soon saw him moving – downwards – to join

Stockport County. At County, however, he was a revelation as he shook off his injury problems and helped Stockport to promotion from the Third Division North. That was enough to persuade Oldham to recruit him but after a couple of seasons at Boundary Park he was on the move again, this time linking up with Nottingham Forest. It was at Forest that he really blossomed, winning his first international cap and coming to the attention of Arsenal in May 1928. Jones was a regular over the next six seasons as the Gunners swept all before them. He claimed three league championship medals and an FA Cup runners-up medal in 214 games for the club. When he came to Arsenal he arrived as a recognised winger but Chapman, in one of his most inspired moves, converted Jones into a wing-half, making him one of the most effective in the league. He won a total of seven Welsh caps between 1926 and 1933, with three of those coming while he was with Arsenal.

JONES, LESLIE. Yet another Welsh Jones who found his way to Highbury via Cardiff City. Jones signed for Cardiff in 1929 and had five years with them before joining Coventry, then a Third Division South side. Jones helped them to the third division title before joining Arsenal in November 1937. In his first season at Highbury he claimed a championship medal but a year later war had broken out and Jones's career came to an effective end. He continued to play for Arsenal during the war years but in 1946 returned home to Wales, joining Swansea on a free transfer. He won his first Welsh cap as a Cardiff player in 1933 and went on to win 11 caps, four of these while he was with Arsenal. In all, he made just 61 appearances for Arsenal but for an inside-forward scored remarkably few goals – just three.

JONSSON, SIGGI. Icelandic international signed from Sheffield Wednesday in 1989. Prior to that he had played with the Icelandic club Akranes before coming to Sheffield Wednesday during the 1984–85 season. He had a loan spell with Barnsley during the 1985–86 season. He retired after a couple of seasons at Highbury following a serious back injury.

JOY, BERNARD. One of the most famous names in the history of Arsenal Football Club as well as amateur football. Joy was born in London and initially played with London University and the Casuals. In 1936 he won an FA Amateur Cup winners medal with the Casuals and also captained the Great Britain football team at the 1936 Olympic Games in Berlin. Joy had also played with Southend United and even had a game with Fulham but signed for Arsenal in May 1935 as an amateur and remained with them until the end of 1946. Between 1934 and 1937 he won ten caps for the England amateur side and in 1936 won a cap for the full England team, becoming the last amateur ever to play for England. In 1938 he picked up a league championship medal with Arsenal and an FA Charity Shield medal. Joy continued to play league football for Arsenal up until the war, making 44 appearances in the 1938–39 season, and then played wartime football with the club, appearing in two wartime Cup finals. After the war he made just 13 appearances in the 1946–47 season before retiring. In all, he played 106 games for the Gunners mainly as a centre-half, but never getting on the score-sheet. He later became a distinguished journalist.

JULIANS, LEN. Joined Arsenal from Leyton Orient in December 1958 in a deal that took Stan Charlton and Tony Biggs in the opposite direction. Julians scored on his home debut but with so much goalscoring talent around Highbury, he always had difficulty in winning a regular place. He played just 24 games, scoring ten goals, before he moved to Nottingham Forest in the summer of 1960 for £10,000. He later had a fine spell with Millwall.

JUVENTUS. Arsenal first played the crack Italian club Juventus in a friendly in November 1958 at Highbury, watched by a crowd of over 51,000. Arsenal won 3–1 and then played them again six months later in Turin. This time Arsenal lost 1–3. They also played them in the semi-final of the European Cup Winners Cup in 1980, drawing 1–1 in Italy but winning 1–0 at Highbury to go through to the final.

K

KELLY, EDDIE. Kelly was a frustrating player who promised much but in the end did not quite deliver. Yet he will always be remembered as the scorer of two of the most crucial goals in the club's history. The first was against Anderlecht in the 1970 Fairs Cup Final second leg, when he hit the goal that set Arsenal on their way to victory. The second came in extra time in the 1971 Cup final when Kelly, on as a substitute, poked a ball through a crowd of players to give Arsenal an equaliser. Charlie George did the rest and Arsenal won the Double. Born in Glasgow, Kelly joined Arsenal as an apprentice in 1966, making his league debut in December 1969 against Sheffield Wednesday. He was as tough a tackler as any to be found in the Football League and could pass the ball with accuracy, but he seemed to lose his appetite for the game and would often go three or four games without contributing much. Injuries also interrupted his career and in September 1976 Arsenal sold him to Queens Park Rangers for £60,000. By then he had made almost 250 appearances for the club, scoring 19 goals. He later had spells with Leicester, Notts County, Bournemouth and Torquay before drifting out of the game. At Highbury he won three Scottish under–23 caps to add to his Scottish youth caps. Full international honours seemed just a short distance away but his inconsistency and lack of commitment meant that they never materialised.

KELSEY, JACK. Welsh international goalkeeper who spent more than ten seasons in the Gunners goal. Kelsey was undoubtedly one of Arsenal's finest ever goalkeepers and, with over 400 appearances to his name, was also one of the club's greatest servants. Born in Wales, he came to Highbury as a junior, signing professional forms in August 1949. But with the great George Swindin still keeping goal for the Gunners, Kelsey was forced to wait until February 1951 before making his league debut. Arsenal lost 5–2 to Charlton Athletic and it seemed that Kelsey might never play again but the Arsenal manager Tom Whittaker refused to blame the youngster and he was soon given a second opportunity. He eventually redeemed himself, though it was not until the 1952–53 season that he finally established himself as first-team choice. From then on he was a permanent fixture between the Highbury posts. He won a league championship medal that season and a Charity Shield medal the next. In 1954 he also won the first of his 41 Welsh caps when he played against Northern Ireland. At one time his 41 caps was a British record for a goalkeeper. In 1958 he was the Welsh goalkeeper at the World Cup finals in Sweden and in 1955 played for Great Britain against the Rest of Europe. Kelsey was a formidable goalkeeper: tall, strong and with an athletic leap. In early 1959 he broke an arm and did not reappear until the autumn of that year. At one point it seemed he might have played his last game for the Gunners but he fought his way back into the side to oust Jim Standen from between the posts. In May 1962, playing for Wales against Brazil in Rio, he severely injured his back diving at the feet of the Brazilian centre-forward Vava. It was an injury that was to end his career. He battled his way back to fitness but it was no use – the cat-like qualities that had made him such an outstanding custodian had gone and he was forced to retire. He had played 414 games for the club. He was later appointed commercial manager of Arsenal, a position he held for many years.

KELSO, PHIL. Arsenal manager 1904–8. After the sensational resignation of Harry Bradshaw as Arsenal won promotion, Kelso was drafted in to be the club's first manager as a first-division side. He had only moderate success, but at least he kept them in the upper division and consolidated their position, which, given the club's financial difficulties, was a not inconsiderable task. But Arsenal's money problems never really disappeared and in 1908, with attendances falling, the financial difficulties became critical once more. Kelso had had enough and at the end of the season resigned and went off to Largs to run a hotel. A year later, however, he was tempted back into the game and was appointed manager of Fulham, a job he held until 1924.

KENNEDY, ANDY. Inter-war defender who formed an Irish international full-back pairing at Highbury with Alex Mackie. Kennedy came to the club from Crystal Palace in 1920, having previously played with Belfast Celtic and Glentoran, but had to wait until December 1922 before he made his debut. He had a couple of seasons as a regular then drifted out of the side, making only the occasional appearance, but he did appear in the 1927 FA Cup final against Cardiff City. In January 1928 he was transferred to Everton and after a couple of seasons at Goodison wound up at Tranmere Rovers.

KENNEDY, RAY. A key member of the Gunners side that clinched the Double in 1971 and the man who scored the goal that clinched the league title for Arsenal against Tottenham. Born in the north-east, Kennedy came to Arsenal as a young apprentice, making his league debut against Sunderland in October 1969. In just a handful of appearances that season he struck four goals, including the first against Anderlecht in the European Fairs Cup final that set Arsenal on their way to victory. The following season he was given his chance early on and eventually made 65 appearances as Arsenal swept aside everything before them. He hit 19 goals in the league and ended the season with a total of 27 goals. With John Radford alongside him, Arsenal were a power to behold, the pair of them almost impossible to contain. Kennedy might not have been the quickest of strikers, nor the most athletic but he was powerful, had a strong shot and could head the ball with accuracy. It seemed he was destined for a long and distinguished Arsenal career. But the following season he had lost his edge. He appeared as substitute in the 1972 FA Cup final and still ended the season with 20 goals. He remained at the club until the summer of 1974 but by then he was showing signs of overweight and seemed to have lost his enthusiasm for Highbury. Arsenal decided to sell him, transferring him to Liverpool for £200,000, Bill Shankly's final signing. At Anfield he continued to flounder until Bob Paisley, in a masterstroke, converted him into a midfielder. Suddenly Kennedy was transformed to become one of the finest midfielders in European football. He went on to win further league championship medals, and European medals and at the end of his Liverpool days was one of the most honoured players in the history of British football. He picked up six England under–23 caps while he was with Arsenal but did not win an England cap until he had joined Liverpool, where he eventually won 17 caps. After Liverpool he had spells with Swansea, helping them gain promotion to the first division, and then had a few games with Hartlepool before retiring. Kennedy then discovered that he had Parkinson's Disease. Some years later Arsenal and Liverpool played a benefit game at Highbury to help raise funds for his medical provision. Kennedy was also forced to sell his vast collection of medals and caps in order to raise money. Although Kennedy's finest days as a player were with Liverpool, there is no doubt that Arsenal fans hold a great affection for him and will always remember the way he leapt above the Spurs defence one warm, spring evening at White Hart Lane to clinch the title.

KEOWN, MARTIN. Now in his second spell with the Gunners. Keown was originally at Highbury as a youngster and was given his chance in 1985, performing splendidly against Liverpool. A tall central defender, he seemed to have a glittering career ahead of him as a partner to David O'Leary but six months later the 19-year-old surprised everyone by failing to agree a new contract with the club. After just 24 games Arsenal sold him to Aston Villa for £125,000. He played over 100 games at Villa, impressing with his powerful defending and was then sold on to Everton. Although Everton provided another fine stage for his talents, he was in a side that was struggling and in February 1993 returned to Highbury in a £2 million deal, perhaps regretful that he had ever left in the first place. Although he was playing in a mediocre side at Everton, Keown always looked impressive and England manager Graham Taylor gave him his opportunity against France in February 1992. He quickly developed an understanding with Des Walker and went on to win further caps. He was one of the few England successes in the European Championships.

KIDD, BRIAN. A European Cup winner with Manchester United, Kidd was bought as a replacement for the departing Ray Kennedy. But the truth was that, although he was still young, his most prolific goalscoring days were already

Brian Kidd

behind him. What's more, he was joining an Arsenal side that was not able to give him the kind of support he needed. Kidd had excelled at Old Trafford with the likes of Law, Best and Charlton surrounding him but at Highbury there was no such richness of talent. He began well enough, with 23 goals in his first season, but after that he was struggling as Arsenal slipped down the table. He played a total of 90 games for the club, finding the net 34 times. In the summer of 1976 he moved to Manchester City and then had a spell with Everton, followed by a period in America. He eventually returned home to manage Preston North End but finished up as a coach at Old Trafford. He was later appointed assistant manager under Alex Ferguson and helped his old club to successive league titles.

KIRCHEN, ALF. Arsenal winger in the years immediately prior to the Second World War. Kirchen came to Highbury from Norwich for £6,000 in March 1935, a not inconsiderable amount considering he had only made 13 appearances for the Canaries, though it was probably the seven goals he had scored that inflated his transfer value. He scored twice on his debut against Tottenham Hotspur, but did not win a regular spot in the side until the 1936–37 season. He won a league championship medal the following season and a Charity Shield winners medal in 1938. Kirchen was a fast, goalscoring winger who in 117 games for the Gunners netted 56 goals. During the war he continued to give service to Arsenal, playing in both Arsenal's wartime Cup finals. In September 1943, playing at West Ham in a wartime game, he injured a knee and was forced to quit the game. He later became a coach at Norwich and a director of the club as well. Kirchen was chosen to tour Scandinavia with the England squad in 1937 and won three caps, scoring a couple of goals. He might well have gone on to win more caps but for the presence of Matthews and Finney. As it was, his only other international honours came in wartime internationals.

KNIGHTON, LESLIE. Appointed manager of Arsenal in 1919 after the club had been given first division status.

Knighton had been assistant manager at Huddersfield Town and then Manchester City before joining Arsenal. His chief task at Arsenal was to keep the club financially stable after its expensive move to Highbury and that meant not signing players. It was a tall order but Knighton persevered, though with little success on the field. Arsenal just about managed to hold their own in the league to begin with, but results eventually deteriorated and the club narrowly avoided relegation twice. Knighton decided to force the hand of the chairman Sir Henry Norris and demanded action to buy new players. Norris refused and instead advertised for a new manager. Knighton, however, found work quickly, joining Bournemouth and then had a highly successful spell with Birmingham City. He also managed Chelsea for a time, as well as Shrewsbury.

KOP Arsenal can claim to be the first club to ever use the word 'kop'. In 1904 at the Manor Ground the club built a new, steeply banked terracing. Many local soldiers who came to the games nicknamed it 'the Kop', after the Spion Kop, where a famous battle had taken place during the Boer War. Hundreds of soldiers had died during the battle for the small hill. Many other clubs, most notably Liverpool, later called their terracings by the same name.

L

LAMBERT, JACK. A member of the great Arsenal side of the 1920s and '30s. He came to Highbury after spells with Rotherham, Leeds United and Doncaster Rovers in June 1926 for £2,000. During his first three years with the club he made few appearances in the first team, even though he had made his league debut shortly after joining. It was not until the 1929–30 season that he secured his place. That season he went on to help the Gunners lift the FA Cup, scoring in the final as Arsenal beat Huddersfield 2–0. Lambert netted 25 goals in all that season. The following season he was even more prolific, setting new goalscoring records at Highbury as he scored 48 goals over the season, 38 of those in the league. By the end of the season Arsenal were league champions in no small part due to Lambert's goals. During the remainder of his days at Arsenal he won an FA Cup runners-up medal and appeared in the Charity Shield. In October 1933 he left Arsenal to join Fulham but after retiring from the game returned to Arsenal to help coach their junior sides. Although Lambert was never one of the first names to trip off the tongue when talking about the great inter-war Arsenal side, it was his goals that were mainly responsible for winning one FA Cup and a league title. He was never capped by his country but made a total of 183 appearances for Arsenal, scoring a remarkable 133 goals.

LAST-MINUTE GOAL. Of all the last-minute goals Arsenal have scored, none was more important or more memorable than Arsenal's last-second goal against Liverpool at Anfield to win the league championship in 1989. The scorer was Michael Thomas, who latched on to a ball from Alan Smith, and raced into the penalty area before drilling a shot beyond the outstretched Bruce Grobbelaar in the Liverpool goal. Arsenal were already leading 1–0 but had to score another goal in order to lift the title. There was barely time to kick off again before the final whistle and Arsenal had stolen the championship from under the noses of Liverpool.

LAWTON, TOMMY. Tommy Lawton was one of the outstanding names in British football, though by the time he arrived at Highbury his career was all but over. Lawton had been born in Bolton and began his football at Burnley but moved to Everton for £6,500 in March 1937. There he teamed up with the greatest goalscorer of them all, Dixie Dean, who took the youngster under his wing and taught him the ways of goalscoring. Lawton was a good pupil, scoring 65 goals in just 87 appearances over the next couple of years. Everton were league champions but then the war intervened, robbing Lawton of his best days. After the war he decided that he did not want to play for Everton again and left to join Chelsea for £14,000. Two seasons later he moved to Notts County for a record fee. He remained there for five years before joining Brentford in March 1952. Eighteen months later Arsenal manager Tom Whittaker brought him to Highbury. Arsenal had made a poor start to the season and needed an inspirational name to give the crowd and the side a lift. Lawton cost Arsenal £10,000 though whether or not he was worth it is debatable. He did not score many goals – 19 in 50 appearances – but no doubt he put a few thousand more on the average gate. He played just three seasons for Arsenal before moving on to Kettering Town as player-manager. In his league career

Tommy Lawton

he had scored 231 goals in 390 games. Lawton won his first England cap in October 1938, having turned 18 only a few days earlier. Although England lost that day, Lawton converted a penalty and went on to play 23 games for his country, his last cap coming ten years later. He scored 22 goals for England and also played in a number of wartime internationals, where he scored 23 goals. Had it not been for the intervention of war, Lawton would almost certainly have been the highest England goalscorer of them all.

LEAGUE CHAMPIONSHIP. Arsenal have won the league championship on ten occasions: 1930–31; 1932–33; 1933–34; 1934–35; 1937–38; 1947–48; 1952–53; 1970–71; 1988–89; 1990–91.

LEAGUE CHAMPIONSHIP – CLOSEST. The league championship of 1988–89 was the closest on record, with Arsenal and Liverpool facing each other at Anfield in a final match of the season decider. Liverpool needed to avoid defeat by two clear goals in order to win not only the championship but also a second double. Victory by two clear goals for Arsenal, however, would take the title to Highbury. It seemed inconceivable that Arsenal could do it but in the event they won 2–0 with a goal in injury time to clinch the championship. Although both sides had equal points and equal goal difference, Arsenal had scored more goals than Liverpool. On the old goal-average system Liverpool would have been champions.

LEAGUE CHAMPIONSHIP HAT TRICK. Arsenal won three successive league titles between 1932 and 1935 to equal the achievement of Huddersfield Town.

LEAGUE CHAMPIONSHIP, RUNNERS-UP. Arsenal have been runners-up on three occasions: 1925–26; 1931–32; 1972–73.

LEAGUE GOALS – CAREER HIGHEST. Cliff Bastin holds the Arsenal record for the highest number of goals, with a career total of 150 achieved between 1930 and 1947.

LEAGUE GOALS – LEAST CONCEDED. During the 1990–91 season Arsenal conceded just 18 goals.

LEAGUE GOALS – MOST INDIVIDUAL. Ted Drake holds the Arsenal record for the most league goals in a season, with 42 scored in the first division during the 1934–35 season.

LEAGUE GOALS – MOST SCORED. Arsenal's highest goal tally in the Football League was during the 1930–31 season, when they scored 127 goals to win their first league championship.

LEAGUE POINTS – HIGHEST. Arsenal's highest league points tally for a season under the two-points-for-a-win rule was 66 in the first division in 1930–31 as they clinched their first league championship. Under the three-points-for-a-win rule their highest tally is 83, achieved in the 1990–91 season, when they also won the championship.

LEAGUE VICTORY – HIGHEST. Arsenal's most impressive league victory was a 12–0 win over Loughborough in a division two game on 12 March 1900.

LEWIS, CHARLIE. Although he was born in Plumstead, Charlie Lewis played his early football with Eltham and Maidstone United. It was not until the summer of 1907, when he was into his early twenties, that he joined Arsenal. He made his league debut later that year in December against Sunderland, scoring twice as the Gunners won 4–0. That was enough to confirm his ability and a first-team place was guaranteed. From then until war interrupted league football, Lewis was a regular, one of the first names on the team sheet. By the time football resumed after the war Lewis was really too old. He had another half dozen games for the club in the years up to 1921 but most of his time was spent in reserve-team football. In the end he decided to quit Arsenal and went off to non-league Margate. Lewis was a forward, as versatile as any on the Arsenal books at the time. His favoured position was as an inside-right but he didn't really mind where he played and could be equally effective on either wing. He played 260 games for Arsenal, scoring 51 goals.

LEWIS, DAN. The very mention of the word Wembley to Dan Lewis was likely to send him into a rage. Poor Lewis was the Arsenal goalkeeper in the 1927 final when a simple shot spun under his arms and into the net for the only goal of the game. Cardiff could hardly believe their good fortune. What's more, Lewis was a Welshman, born not far from Cardiff, and there were plenty of suspicious Arsenal supporters who wondered if perhaps his Welsh origins might have had something to do with his fumbling fingers. Three years later Arsenal reached the final again and this time Lewis was ready to show his real worth but unfortunately tragedy struck and he was injured just weeks before the final. In six seasons at Arsenal Lewis made only 188 appearances. He was never a regular but was in and out of the side, depending on injury and form. Yet he was generally thought to be a more than reliable keeper. He won three Welsh caps while he was an Arsenal player.

LEWIS, REG. Reg Lewis was another of the many players whose careers were interrupted by war. He had joined Arsenal in 1935 as a youngster, turning professional two years later. By then he had already played for the first team, although he did not make his league debut until January 1938. He was just coming into his stride and getting regular first-team football when war broke out and he found himself enrolled in the army. But when duties permitted he did manage to pull on the Arsenal shirt for an occasional wartime game. His most memorable was probably in the Football League Cup South final when he struck four goals as Arsenal thrashed Charlton Athletic 7–1 at Wembley. After the war he was back into the Arsenal side, scoring 29 league goals in just 28 appearances in his first season. The following season, 1947–48, Arsenal were champions, with Lewis netting 14 league goals. In 1950 it was Lewis who masterminded Arsenal's FA Cup triumph over Liverpool with two goals. By then he was getting on and his appearances after the Cup final victory became infrequent. He eventually retired at the end of the 1952–1953 season, though he had taken no part in Arsenal's league championship of that season. He played 214 games, scoring 158 goals for Arsenal. He was capped twice for England B in 1950 and also played in the England-Scotland game to raise money for the Bolton Disaster Fund but this game was not recognised as a full international.

LIMPAR, ANDERS. Swedish international signed from the Italian club Cremonese for £1.3 million. Limpar had previously played with Orgryte in Sweden and then Young Boys of Berne. He slotted into the English game as if he had played there all his life, bringing added flair and pace to the Arsenal midfield. He was a joy to watch with his bounty of skills. Limpar arrived with the reputation of a ball player but not a goalscorer. Yet he soon became a regular scorer. He hit a hat trick against Coventry City in the final game of the 1990/91 season. Limpar was a member of Arsenal's championship side of 1990–91 but then faded slightly and found himself sidelined. Eventually, he opted for a transfer to Everton in March 1994.

LINIGHAN, ANDY. Andy Linighan had certainly done the rounds before he arrived at Highbury. He began with Hartlepool United and then moved to Leeds United during the summer of 1984. He had a good spell with Leeds and was an ever-present but was then sold to Oldham Athletic 18 months later for just £65,000 – a third of what Leeds had paid for him. At Boundary Park he truly began to shine and, with a number of first division clubs casting their eye over him, Norwich jumped in with a £350,000 bid that took him to Carrow Road, as a replacement for Steve Bruce, who had just been sold to Manchester United. Linighan was a huge success as Norwich put up a genuine fight for the championship. He spent two years there, missing just a couple of games, before Arsenal came in with a £1.25 million offer in June 1990. Since then Linighan has not always been a regular, especially with Steve Bould and

Tony Adams in such devastating form. But he came into his own in the FA Cup final of 1993, scoring the last-minute goal that brought the Cup to Highbury. He had earlier won a winners medal in the Coca-Cola Cup final.

LISHMAN, DOUG. Post-war goalscorer who played a vital role in Arsenal's league championship triumph. Birmingham-born Lishman was an amateur footballer before the war who joined up with Walsall immediately after hostilities ceased. In just 59 appearances for Walsall he scored 26 goals and soon had every club in the land after his services. Arsenal won the race and in May 1948 he was signed for £10,500. Over the next eight seasons he would give valuable service, scoring 173 goals in 300 games. He was essentially an inside-left but he liked the freedom to roam, often cutting in from the left wing or taking up a central position. He was in the side virtually from the start, making his debut against Sheffield United early in the new season, 1948–49. He went on to score 24 goals that season. Unfortunately, injury cut short his appearances the following season as Arsenal went on to lift the FA Cup. Lishman played no part in the proceedings, managing just 14 league appearances. His best season was 1951–52 when Arsenal finished in third spot and also reached the Cup final, with Lishman scoring 35 goals, including 23 in the league. He also scored three hat tricks in succession at Highbury that season. The following season, as Arsenal won the championship, Lishman netted 22 league goals and 29 in all. With all those goals Lishman might have expected some international recognition but it never really came. All he received was a call-up as an England reserve, one England B cap, and a game for the Football league against the Danish league. In March 1956 he left Arsenal to join Nottingham Forest but retired a year later.

LITTLEWOODS CUP. See Football League Cup.

LOGIE, JIMMY. One of the great post-war Scottish players and one of the finest ever to play for Arsenal. Although Logie was born in Edinburgh, he was never spotted by any

Jimmy Logie

of the major Scottish clubs and came to Arsenal just before the outbreak of the Second World War. Unfortunately, his career was to be severely interrupted by the war and he did not make his league debut until the 1946–47 season. Had Logie been playing league football during those years, he might well have matured into the finest of all Scottish players. As it was, he was to be a major influence on the Arsenal side of the late 1940s and early '50s. He was a member of the 1950 Cup-winning side that beat Liverpool at Wembley and also in the side that lost the 1952 final to Newcastle. Logie also picked up two league championship medals with the 1948 and 1953 sides. In all, he played getting on for 400 games for the club, netting a total of 86 goals. Logie was a typical Scottish forward; plastered hair, parting down the middle, adept and a skilful dribbler. Strangely, he was capped only once by his country, in October 1952, when Scotland played Northern Ireland. Quite why he should win just the one cap remains a mystery as there is little doubt that Logie was worth a great many more honours. After all, he had captained Arsenal and had helped inspire them to the greatest honours in the English game. In February 1955 he decided to leave Highbury, joining non-league Gravesend, but he retired from football four years later.

LONGEST GAMES. One of the most remarkable series of games Arsenal ever played was against Leicester City during the 1974–75 season, when the two clubs met on no less than seven occasions. They met twice in the league and then played two games in the League Cup, with Leicester winning. Then in February 1975 they faced each other three times in the fifth round of the FA Cup before Arsenal went through to the next round. The longest game of all, however, came in the third round of the FA Cup in January 1979 when Arsenal were drawn against Sheffield Wednesday at Hillsborough. In all, it took five games to decide the tie. The first game was drawn 1–1. In the replay at Highbury the two sides again drew 1–1 after extra time. The third game was played at Filbert Street and, after extra time, finished 2–2. The fourth game was also played at

Filbert Street, this time finishing 3–3 after extra time. In the fifth game Arsenal finally won 2–0, in a match once more played at Filbert Street. It had taken Arsenal 540 minutes to finally overcome them.

LUKIC, JOHN. Born in Chesterfield, the home of great goalkeepers, Lukic began his football with Leeds United as a schoolboy. He later signed professional forms and made his debut for Leeds against Valetta in the UEFA Cup in October 1979. He went on to play 146 successive games for Leeds, a club record, but after asking for a transfer he was dropped and missed the second half of the 1982–83 season. At the end of that season Arsenal paid £75,000 for his services as cover for Pat Jennings. He eventually took over from Jennings in 1985. Two years later he played in the League Cup final as Arsenal beat Liverpool. Then in the 1988–89 season he was the Arsenal goalkeeper as the club took the league title, an ever-present throughout the campaign. He had one more year at Highbury but when, in the summer of 1990, Arsenal signed David Seaman he realised he was about to become the second-string goalkeeper again. And so he moved back to Leeds for £100,000. Two years later he was the winner of another league championship medal, this time with Leeds. In all he played more than 270 games for Arsenal.

LYDERSEN, PAL. The Norwegian international cost Arsenal £500,000 when he moved from Start Kristiansud in 1991. A full-back, he is also reputed to possess one of the hardest shots at Highbury. He can also play as a left-back or even as a sweeper.

M

MACAULAY, ARCHIE. Prior to the Second World War Macaulay was a star with Glasgow Rangers, winning league and Cup honours before he signed for West Ham in 1937. Immediately after the war he joined Brentford but at the end of his first season they were relegated and Macaulay moved to Highbury in July 1947 for £10,000. Earlier that year he had won his first Scottish cap and had also played for Great Britain against the Rest of Europe. The signing of Macaulay was something of a coup and by the end of his first season he had picked up a championship medal. Further international honours came his way as he continued to impress with his displays at inside-forward. He was as cultured as they come, skilful and with a touch of pace. By 1950, however, he was getting on and was beginning to lose his touch. He was left out of the FA Cup final side and then decided to try his luck elsewhere. He moved to Fulham and later had spells managing Dundee, West Brom, Norwich and Brighton.

McCLELLAND, JACK. Second-string Arsenal goalkeeper of the early 1960s. He joined Arsenal from Glenavon in October 1960 for just £7,000. A week later he won his first international cap but was nowhere near as successful with the Arsenal. When Jack Kelsey was injured he managed 34 consecutive games but then broke a collar bone and found himself marginalised yet again. During the summer of 1964 he signed for Fulham. He was capped five times for Northern Ireland while an Arsenal player.

McCULLOUGH, BILLY. Came to Arsenal from Portadown for £5,000 along with Jimmy Magill in September 1958. He was an aggressive full-back who soon became a regular in the side. He went on to play 268 games for the club and was capped nine times by Northern Ireland while he was at Arsenal. In 1965 he lost his spot to Peter Storey and went off to join Millwall. He later went into management and had the unique distinction of managing both the Republic of Ireland and Northern Ireland.

McDERMOTT, BRIAN. Former England youth international who made his debut against Bristol City in March 1979. He played just 44 games for the Gunners upfront, then moved to Oxford United at the end of 1984 for £40,000.

MacDONALD, MALCOLM. When Malcolm Macdonald signed for Arsenal for £333,000 in August 1976 he smashed the British transfer record. He was the hottest property in British football, having scored 121 goals in 228 games for Newcastle. The Geordies loved him and when he joined Arsenal there were protests throughout Newcastle at the club's decision to sell. At Highbury they were delighted and much was expected of Macdonald. Unfortunately it never quite materialised as injury brought a premature end to what could have been a dazzling career for the Gunners. He began brilliantly, slamming in 42 goals in his first season with 25 of those coming in the league. In his second season he struck 31 but began to experience problems with his knee. Early in the 1978–79 season he exacerbated the injury and never played football again. It was a great loss to Arsenal. He had played just 130 games but had scored an impressive 75 goals. Macdonald was a bustling, old-fashioned kind of centre-forward. He loved to power into

Malcom Macdonald

penalty areas, the ball at his feet, his foot drawn back like the trigger on a gun, ready to blast the ball into the net. He had tremendous pace and once he was in flow was always difficult to dispossess. Macdonald unfortunately had a habit of telling opposition teams what he was going to do to them. It didn't always come off and on occasion rebounded on him. He may not have been so popular with opposition terraces but at Newcastle and Arsenal, Supermac was an idol. He won his first England cap in May 1972 and went on to collect 14 caps, even scoring five goals for his country against Cyprus. Yet despite all the goals Supermac never won any of the game's major honours. He appeared in three Cup finals but was on the losing side each time. After Arsenal he went into management, first with his old club Fulham and then with Huddersfield, but it never worked out.

McEACHRANE, RODERICK. At one time McEachrane held the record as Arsenal's longest-serving player and, with 393 appearances to his name, had also played more games for Arsenal than any other man. He joined the club from West Ham in May 1902, finally retiring at the end of the 1913–14 season. During that time he helped Arsenal into the first division and was also around, though he played few games, as Arsenal tumbled back into the second division in 1913.

McGOLDRICK, EDDIE. Born in London, McGoldrick was originally a winger but is now more at home as an attacking midfielder or even as a full-back. He played with a variety of non-league clubs before joining Northampton Town during the 1986 close season. He went straight into the side and by the end of his first season had won a fourth division championship medal. After a couple of seasons at the County Ground he signed for Crystal Palace for £200,000. In his first season he found himself in the play-offs, helping Palace to promotion, but was then injured and spent much of the next season sidelined. He came back into the side during the 1990–91 season to enjoy a couple of impressive seasons with Palace before joining Arsenal.

He won his first cap for the Republic of Ireland in 1992 against Switzerland and came on as an 87th minute substitute in the European Cup Winners Cup final against Parma. McGoldrick has never been able to establish himself in the Gunners side and has been regarded as a utility player, never quite sure of his best position.

McKINNON, ANGUS. Scottish half-back who played just over 250 games for the Gunners between 1908 and 1922. McKinnon was a member of the Arsenal side that was relegated in 1913. He returned to the club after the war when they were back in the first division and helped consolidate their position. He left to join Charlton Athletic in 1922.

MacLEOD, JOHNNY. A major signing from Hibernian during the summer of 1961 for £40,000. MacLeod had attracted considerable attention in Scotland and much was expected of him but it never really worked out. At times he showed touches of class and looked worth his huge transfer fee, but more often his contributions amounted to little. His one claim to fame is that he was the first Arsenal man to score in European competition. He played 112 games for the club but only managed 28 goals, hardly an impressive strike rate for a supposed goalscorer. Before he came to Highbury he had won four Scottish caps but failed to add any more to his collection. In September 1964 he was transferred to Aston Villa for £35,000.

McLINTOCK, FRANK. Mention the 1971 Double side and almost the first name to trip off the tongue will be Frank McLintock. McLintock was skipper of the side and one of the best in the club's history. He was a powerhouse in the midfield; a tenacious tackler, uncompromising, brave, the man to have on your side when the going gets tough. Born in Glasgow, he had begun his footballing career with Leicester City in January 1957 and was twice on the losing side in an FA Cup final with them. He left the Midlands to join Arsenal in October 1964, with Billy Wright paying £80,000 for his services. He then played in two losing League Cup finals with Arsenal and must have wondered

Frank McLintock

if he would ever be on the winning side at Wembley. McLintock had done well at Highbury as a wing-half but in the 1969–70 season, with injuries mounting, coach Don Howe suggested moving the Scot into the centre of the defence. McLintock was reluctant but he was a revelation and was soon showing the inspirational leadership that would serve the Gunners well over the next few years. In 1970 they lifted the European Fairs Cup, then the following year clinched the League and Cup double. That same year he was named as Footballer of the Year and not long after was made an MBE. There was little doubt that McLintock was Arsenal's driving force on the field. His refusal to give in was crucial in the closing games of Arsenal's Double season, especially during the Cup final as the Gunners went a goal down to Liverpool. In April 1973 McLintock was allowed to leave Highbury, signing for Queens Park Rangers for a bargain £25,000. Fans were in uproar, especially as McLintock then continued to give QPR the same kind of inspired leadership as he had given Arsenal, Rangers coming within a whisker of winning the title. After QPR McLintock, not surprisingly, turned his hand to management, having spells with his old club Leicester and then Brentford.

McNAB, BOB. Born in Huddersfield, Bob McNab first played with Huddersfield Town, making over 60 appearances for the Yorkshire side and winning himself a reputation as one of the finest full-backs outside of the first division. The big clubs were queuing up to buy him and, although Liverpool were favourites, Bertie Mee nipped in with a £50,000 record offer for a full-back in October 1966 and McNab was off to Highbury. He was an instant hit, going on to make more than 400 appearances for the Gunners. McNab was a tenacious tackler but with enough flair and pace to bring the ball confidently out of defence. In 1968 and 1969 he was in the Gunners side in two losing League Cup finals but at least he won his first England cap, coming on as a substitute in the goalless draw with Romania. He would go on to win another three caps. But, perhaps more important, the following season he won his first major medal as Arsenal won the European Fairs Cup. The next season it was the Double. In 1972 he played in the FA Cup final against Leeds United and then two years later was give a free transfer, joining Wolverhampton Wanderers. By then he was 32 years old and Sammy Nelson had taken over the left-back slot. But it had been a glorious career and he is remembered by fans as part of one of the finest defences the club has ever had.

MAGILL, JIMMY. Irish full-back signed from Portadown along with Billy McCullough for £5,000 in September 1958. Magill made his debut for Arsenal in December 1959, with the Gunners on the wrong end of a 5–1 thrashing. But he held on to his place until Don Howe came along. That was the signal for Magill to call it a day and he left to join Brighton for £6,000. But while he was not always the most popular of players at Highbury he was certainly rated by the Northern Irish, who capped him 21 times during his Arsenal days. He later managed in Denmark.

MALE, GEORGE. One of the finest full-backs of the interwar years. Male was not only captain of Arsenal but also captain of England, skippering them on six occasions. He won 19 caps for his country, his first against Italy in 1934 in the famous game at Highbury. His final England cap came shortly before war broke out, in May 1939 against Romania. With his England partner Eddie Hapgood alongside him in the Arsenal side as well, the Gunners defence was almost impregnable. It was little wonder the club won so many honours with such sure men at the back. Male came to Highbury while he was still young, signing professional forms in May 1930. Seven months later he made his debut against Blackpool, although it would be another couple of seasons before he fully established himself. By 1932 he was a regular, going on to win four league championship medals, an FA Cup winners medal and a losers medal in 1932. The 1932 final against Newcastle was, in fact, his FA Cup debut. Male was still around after the war and even played eight games during the 1947–48 championship season, though not quite enough to earn himself a fifth championship medal. He retired at the end of that season and took up an appointment as youth-team coach, a job he held until his eventual retirement in May 1975. By then he had been around Highbury for 45 years, one of the club's finest ever servants.

MANAGER. Since its inception, Arsenal Football Club has had only 16 managers, a low number by the standards of most Football League clubs. They have been as follows:
1897–98 T. B. Mitchell
1898–99 George Elcoat
1899–1904 Harry Bradshaw
1904–8 Phil Kelso
1908–15 George Morrell
1919–25 Leslie Knighton
1925–34 Herbert Chapman
1934–47 George Allison
1947–56 Tom Whittaker
1956–58 Jack Crayston
1958–62 George Swindin
1962–66 Billy Wright
1966–76 Bertie Mee
1976–83 Terry Neill
1983–86 Don Howe
1986–   George Graham

MANAGER OF THE YEAR. George Graham won the award for Manager of the Year in 1989 and 1991, after Arsenal had won the league championship. Prior to that, Bertie Mee won the award in 1971 after Arsenal had clinched the league and Cup double.

MANCINI, TERRY. Terry Mancini, with his Max Wall haircut and galloping style, was an unmistakable character at Highbury. Born in London, Mancini came to Arsenal from Queens Park Rangers for £20,000 in October 1974. Prior to that he had played with Watford and with Port Elizabeth in South Africa. Plenty of eyebrows were raised when Terry Neill signed him. Mancini was then 32 years of age, a time when most footballers are thinking about hanging up their boots. But not Mancini. Even though he might have looked his age, if not even older, he was always full of enthusiasm. He was like a breath of fresh air and also had years of experience to pass on to the youngsters. He slotted into the centre of the defence and for two seasons performed heroically. Then in September 1976, at the age of 34, he joined Aldershot on a free transfer. Despite being born in London, Mancini qualified to play for the Republic of Ireland, winning five caps between 1974 and 1975.

MANOR GROUND. Home of Arsenal from 1888 to 1890 and 1893 to 1913.

MARINELLO, PETER. The newspapers labelled him the new George Best and his early career certainly showed the kind of touches that Best boasted. Marinello began his football with Hibernian, winning rave notices. Then at the age of 19 he was tempted south of the border in a massive £100,000 transfer. The long-haired Marinello made his Arsenal debut at Old Trafford, of all places, and scored a sensational goal after a 50-yard run through the entire United defence. It was little wonder the papers went over-board. What with that and his £100,000 tag, Marinello found too much pressure resting on his young shoulders. His form deteriorated and he soon found himself out of the team. Then followed a serious knee injury and all the hopes that he was to be the new George Best were dashed. In the end he joined Portsmouth for £80,000, a sad end to what had been such a promising start. There was a lesson for everybody in the Marinello story.

MARINER, PAUL. Mariner came to Highbury late in his career. He had already starred with Plymouth Argyle and Ipswich but with Charlie Nicholas and Tony Woodcock not providing the goals, it was thought that Mariner might inspire them to greater deeds. And so in February 1984 manager Don Howe signed him from Ipswich for £150,000. He was probably worth the gamble but in truth was little different than Nicholas or Woodcock. What was really needed was someone to scheme those goals for the front runners. Mariner was the England centre-forward with 33 caps to his name and was to win a couple more while he was at Highbury. He began well enough and by the end of the season had scored seven goals in 15 appearances. But the next season the goals dried up and younger players were knocking on the door. It was time to dispense with at least one of the club's expensive international centre-forwards and Mariner was duly despatched to Portsmouth on a free transfer.

MARWOOD, BRIAN. Born in the north-east, Marwood kicked off his footballing days with Hull City before moving to Sheffield Wednesday, where he began to make his mark. He made more than 120 appearances for the Owls before George Graham paid £600,000 to bring him to Highbury in March 1988. The following season he was in the thick of it as Arsenal's assault on the league title took shape. A skilful right-winger, Marwood had pace as well as ability and was soon an effective cog in the Gunners midfield. By the end of his first season he had a league championship medal to show for his endeavours and also an England cap after coming on as a substitute against Saudi Arabia. Injuries then began to interfere with his career. He missed some of the final games of the championship season and then found himself sidelined again the next season. Anders Limpar also came to the club and Marwood's role at Highbury became questionable. In September 1990 he decided to move on, joining Sheffield United for £350,000. He was a player who had been bought to do a specific job and who had done it well, but when others appeared to perform the task with even more efficiency he was discarded.

MEADE, RAPHAEL. Scored with his first touch on his debut in September 1981 in a UEFA Cup game against Panathanaikos. Meade looked to be the answer to all Arsenal's problems but his early goalscoring form soon evaporated and he found himself out of favour though he did suffer more than his fair share of injuries. In five seasons at Highbury he managed just 32 games but scored an impressive 16 goals, a strike rate which suggests that perhaps Arsenal ought to have persevered a little more with him. But he was always something of a lightweight player, never really getting 'stuck in'. In 1985 he was transferred to Sporting Lisbon of Portugal.

MEE, BERTIE. Arsenal manager 1966–76. Mee's footballing career was hardly worth writing home about. He played as a winger with Derby County and then Mansfield Town but was forced into early retirement through injury. He then spent some time in the army, later qualifying as a physiotherapist, and went on to spend 12 years working as a rehabilitation officer to disabled servicemen. He could never have even dared dream that one day he would find himself back in the game, let alone go on to become one of the greatest managers in Arsenal's history. In August 1960 he applied for a job as physio and trainer at Highbury. He was accepted and spent the next six years working in that capacity but clearly impressing enough on the coaching side to be formally appointed manager after Billy Wright had been fired. Nobody outside Highbury knew Mee but it was typical of Arsenal to make such an appointment. New players were quickly added to the squad that season, including Bob McNab and George Graham. Success soon followed. In 1968 they reached the League Cup final, only to be beaten by Leeds United. They repeated the feat the following season, this time going down to Swindon. It was a depressing result and enough to have got some managers the sack, but Mee and his side came bouncing back and a year later had won the European Fairs Cup, the first major trophy at Highbury since 1953. The next year Arsenal clinched the league and Cup double and Mee was hailed as one of the greatest managers in the club's history, having achieved something which even the great Herbert Chapman had never managed. He was also named as Manager of the Year. But that, surprisingly, was the end of the trophies. Arsenal did come within a whisker of winning the FA Cup in 1972 when they lost to Leeds in the final and were also runners-up in the league in 1973. By then Mee was getting

Bertie Mee

older and the pressures of managing at the top were beginning to tell. The team was in decline and needed rebuilding and that was a task even beyond Mee. In March 1976 he announced that he would be retiring at the end of the season. After a break he came back into the game in the less-pressured job as general manager of Watford.

MERCER, JOE. One of the great names in the history of Arsenal Football Club. Mercer was born in Ellesmere Port on Merseyside and first starred with Everton. He won a league championship medal with them in 1939, having won his first England cap a year earlier. He won a total of five caps for his country before war broke out and then went on to win 26 caps in wartime internationals but, surprisingly, never won any further international recognition after the war. When hostilities ceased he returned to Everton but found himself with a knee injury and generally out of favour at Goodison. He was angry and promptly joined Arsenal for £7,000 in November 1946. Eighteen months later Arsenal were league champions. Wing-half Mercer was the inspiration behind the post-war Arsenal side, skippering them to further success in the 1950 FA Cup final when they beat Liverpool, the team with which he did most of his training. Two years later he was back at Wembley as Arsenal went down to Newcastle United, but then crowned his career with another championship in 1953. A year later he broke a leg playing against Liverpool at Highbury and was stretchered off. It was the end of his footballing career. Mercer then turned to management, beginning with Sheffield United. From there he went to Aston Villa, guiding them into the first division and a League Cup triumph. That prompted Manchester City to offer him a job at Maine Road, where he revived a slumbering giant of a club, bringing league championship, FA Cup and European glory to the side. Mercer also had a spell as caretaker manager of England, a period fondly remembered for his uninhibited approach to attacking football. Mercer was one of the most liked men in the game with a smile and a word for anyone. He played almost 300 games for the Gunners. In 1950 he was voted Footballer of the Year and was later awarded the OBE.

Joe Mercer

MERSON, PAUL. Came up through the Arsenal youth system and made his league debut at Highbury in November 1986, coming on as a substitute for Niall Quinn. He had a brief loan spell with Brentford in early 1987. Merson scored in his first full game for the Gunners, finally breaking into the side during the 1988–89 season. He played 37 games that season, scoring ten goals and at the end of it collected a league championship medal. He was also named as PFA Young Player of the Year. Two years later he collected a second championship medal and has since collected an FA Cup winners medal, a League Cup winners medal and a European Cup Winners Cup medal. He was the scorer of Arsenal's first goal in the League Cup final against

Paul Merson

Sheffield Wednesday. The England manager Graham Taylor spotted his potential and he was called up for the England side to face Germany in 1992, coming on as a substitute. He was also selected for the European Championships and has now won more than a dozen caps for his country. Merson has now shifted from a central-attacking position to a wider role and, with his explosive running, has been creating chances for Ian Wright. He has a fierce shot and has notched up well over 50 goals for the club.

MILK CUP. See Football League Cup.

MILLER, ALAN. Arsenal's current second-string goalkeeper. Born in Epping, he was the first player from the FA School of Excellence to win England under-21 honours. He made four appearances during the 1992–93 season but, with David Seaman looking so secure in the Gunners goal, Miller may have some time to wait before he enjoys more regular first-team football.

MILNE, BILLY. During the First World War Billy Milne, who was a sergeant in the Seaforth Highlanders, was awarded the DCM for gallantry in France. Before the war he had played most of his football in Scotland but in August 1921 joined Arsenal. His footballing career at Highbury was one of mixed fortunes, however, and after a broken leg in 1925 he was forced to give up playing. Instead, he turned his attention to coaching and in 1927 was appointed assistant trainer to Tom Whittaker. He continued in that job until the outbreak of the Second World War. In 1947, when Whittaker was appointed manager, Milne was promoted to become first-team trainer. He was also trainer to the England side for a time. He retired in 1960, having given almost 40 years service to the club.

MITCHELL, T. B. Arsenal's first ever manager. Mitchell came to Arsenal in 1897 from Blackburn Rovers but lasted for less than a year at Plumstead. He introduced some fine players to the club and Arsenal rose impressively up the table but in the face of increasing financial problems Mitchell resigned.

MORRELL, GEORGE. Manager of Arsenal 1908–15. Born in Glasgow, Morrell was a qualified referee who had also played junior football. At one time he held a position with Glasgow Rangers but in 1905 was appointed manager of Morton, a club he helped out of financial difficulties. It was hardly surprising, then, that Woolwich Arsenal, also in financial trouble, should look to Morrell to help solve their problems. He arrived in 1908 but was immediately forced to sell some of the club's better-known players. Yet he also bought wisely, bringing in Alf Common and Leigh Roose. But the financial problems got no easier and in the end he was forced to sell even those players he had signed. In 1913 the club were relegated with one of the poorest records of all time. Morrell, however, did oversee the move to Highbury, even though that also turned out to be a source of crippling debt for many years. Promotion never came and when war broke out and the club put up its shutters Morrell resigned.

MORROW, STEVE. Will always be remembered as the man who broke his arm celebrating Arsenal's League Cup victory in 1993. Arsenal first spotted him as a 14-year-old in Northern Ireland and brought him to Highbury in July 1987. Morrow made his debut for Northern Ireland even before he had played for the Gunners, coming on a substitute against Uruguay in May 1990. He spent various periods away from Highbury on loan to Reading, Watford and Barnet. He finally made his breakthrough into the Arsenal side during the 1992–93 season, and went on to score the winning goal against Sheffield Wednesday in the League Cup final. His freak accident after that game, however, sidelined him for the rest of the season so that he missed out on Arsenal's Cup final victory. But he was back in the side for the 1993–94 season and ended it with a winners medal from the European Cup Winners Cup final. A hard tackler and a committed man-to-man marker, Morrow has now played more than a dozen games for Northern Ireland.

MORTENSEN, STAN. Although the great Blackpool and England centre-forward was never officially an Arsenal player, he did guest for the club during the war, in the 1944–45 season, and was remarkably prolific. In 12 appearances in the Football League South he netted 18 goals and in five appearances in the Football League Cup South he scored seven goals. He hit three hat tricks during the season.

MOSCOW DYNAMO. Arsenal played the top Soviet side Moscow Dynamo in November 1945 when Dynamo came to England to play a series of friendly matches. Against an Arsenal side that also included Stan Mortensen and Stanley Matthews, Dynamo won 4–3. The Russians had earlier protested strongly, arguing that this was not Arsenal but England they were facing. The game was played at White Hart Lane in an appalling fog with a crowd of more than 56,000 turning up.

MOSS, FRANK. Arsenal goalkeeper of the 1930s. Born near Preston, Moss began his footballing career with the famous Preston North End but after a couple of seasons was given a free transfer. He joined Oldham Athletic, where again he did not have the best of luck, finding himself as understudy to the England keeper, Jack Hacking. It was almost impossible to break into the side but in November 1931 he was spotted by Herbert Chapman and duly joined Arsenal for £3,000. If others had doubts about Moss, Chapman certainly did not and he went straight into the first team, where he remained for the next four seasons. During that time Moss won three consecutive league championship medals and in April 1934 won his first England cap. He would eventually pick up four caps. In March 1935 he dislocated a shoulder playing in goal at Everton and was forced to go out on the wing, where he scored in Arsenal's 2–0 victory. A year later the shoulder injury recurred and Moss was forced to give up the game. In all, he had played 175 games for the Arsenal. He later became manager of Heart of Midlothian.

MOVIE. In 1939 Arsenal starred in a full-length feature film called *The Arsenal Stadium Mystery*. Excerpts were shot on 6 May 1939 as Arsenal played Brentford at Highbury. Brentford played in an unusual strip that day and were known as The Trojans. Several Arsenal personalities took part in the film, including Cliff Bastin, Tom Whittaker and George Allison.

NEILL, TERRY. Arsenal manager and player. Born in
Northern Ireland in 1942, Terry Neill began his playing
career with the Welsh club Bangor City but left to join
Arsenal in December 1959. A wing-half, he became one of
the youngest ever Arsenal captains and went on to make
241 league appearances for the club. He appeared in the
1968 Cup final as substitute. By then his appearances were
becoming limited and in June 1970 he joined second division Hull City as player-manager. He won his first cap for
Northern Ireland in 1961 against Italy and went on to
make 59 appearances for his country. Not only was he
captain of Northern Ireland, but he also had a spell as
manager. In September 1974 Tottenham appointed him
as their new manager and after some success he returned
to Highbury for the start of the 1976–77 season to take
over from Bertie Mee. His first move as the new Arsenal
manager was to sign Malcolm Macdonald for a record
£333,000. But there were early problems at Highbury,
including public rows with players and a string of poor
results. It was not until Don Howe was brought in as his
assistant that things began to improve. These included a
Wembley appearance in 1978 against Ipswich and then
a more successful appearance in the FA Cup final the fol-

Terry Neill

lowing year, when they beat Manchester United 3–2. In 1980 they reached the final again, this time losing 0–1 to West Ham United. That season Arsenal also reached the final of the European Cup Winners Cup, losing on penalties to Valencia. Unfortunately, that was to mark the end of Arsenal's run of honours. Over the next few seasons all that they had to show for their endeavours were a couple of semi-finals and some respectable league positions. With Don Howe in the wings as a ready-made replacement, Neill was sacked in December 1983.

NELSON, SAMMY. One of the club's finest servants of the 1970s, with more than 400 games. Nelson was a Belfast boy who signed for the Gunners on his 17th birthday in April 1966. He was originally a winger but soon converted to full-back, going on to form one of the club's greatest defensive partnerships with Pat Rice. He and Rice were also international partners. Consistent and dependable, he won his first cap for Northern Ireland in April 1970 after just a handful of appearances for Arsenal and went on to win 48 caps while he was with the club. He made his Arsenal debut in October 1969 against Ipswich and went on to win an FA Cup winners medal in 1979 and losers medals in 1978 and 1980. He also played in the 1980 European Cup Winners Cup final against Valencia. In September 1981 he left Highbury and joined Brighton, where he played for two more seasons before retiring.

NICHOLAS, CHARLIE. In 1983 Charlie Nicholas was the most wanted man in British football. England's top clubs were falling over themselves for his services. In the end it came down to three clubs: Arsenal, Manchester United and Liverpool. Liverpool were favourites but Nicholas, surprisingly, chose Highbury. The fee was £650,000. Born in Glasgow, Nicholas signed for Glasgow Celtic in March 1979 and began a glorious career that brought him to the attention of every scout in British football. He scored 48 goals in 74 league appearances for Celtic, won two championship medals and a League Cup winners medal. In March 1983 he also picked up his first Scottish caps to add to his youth and under-21

Charlie Nicholas

honours. Life at Highbury, however, was not to be so filled with honours. He began promisingly but like others before him he found life in London a distraction. But there were some moments to treasure, such as his two winning goals in the 1987 Littlewoods Cup final against Liverpool. Nicholas was undoubtedly an outstanding player but it may well have to be admitted that a move to Arsenal was, in hindsight, not the best decision for him. In the end George Graham tired of him and in January 1988 he returned to Scotland, joining Aberdeen for £400,000. He later rejoined Celtic. As an Arsenal player Nicholas won 13 Scottish caps. He played 210 games for the Gunners, scoring 67 goals.

NICHOLAS, PETER. Began his Arsenal career in devastating form. He arrived as an expensive emergency recruit, costing £400,000 from Crystal Palace, in March 1981 and immediately brought some much needed bite to the Arsenal midfield. A poor run was suddenly ended with the Gunners shooting up the table to eventually finish in third place. Nicholas continued to give a couple more seasons of splendid service but then found himself sidelined as George Graham brought in some of his youngsters. In October 1983, just two-and-a-half years after he had joined the club, he went back to Crystal Palace for £150,000. He had played 77 games and his only honours came in the shape of international caps for Wales, a total of 17 while he was at Highbury. He would, however, go on to collect more than 70 caps for his country, making him at one point the most capped Welsh player in history.

NICKNAME. Arsenal's nickname is usually 'The Gunners', a name given to them for their association with the munitions factory at Dial Square at Woolwich Arsenal, where a number of those involved with the club worked.

NORRIS, SIR HENRY. Self-made millionaire who was the driving force behind the club for many years. Norris had previously been chairman of Fulham Football Club but came to Arsenal in 1910. It was Norris who secured Arsenal a place in the newly enlarged first division after the First World War and who also engineered the move to High-

bury. Norris lent money to the club and, in bringing Herbert Chapman to Highbury, helped turn Arsenal into the
most famous side in the world. Norris was also a former
Mayor of Fulham and a Member of Parliament.

NORTH BANK. The North Bank was developed in 1931
and when full could hold 17,000 spectators. Prior to that it
had been an insubstantial terracing. But the redevelopment
made the banking considerably higher. Local inhabitants
were even asked to bring all their rubbish as a contribution.
One local coal merchant, eager to help, turned up and
backed his horse and cart just a little too near to a hole
that had been dug to lay some foundations. Unfortunately,
both the horse and cart slipped into the hole. The poor
animal was so badly hurt that it had to be shot and to this
day its remains lie beneath the North Bank. During the
1930s Herbert Chapman had a clock erected on the North
Bank, much to the annoyance of the Football Association.
When the North Bank was roofed in 1935 the clock was
removed and placed at the opposite end of the ground.
During the war the North Bank roof was damaged by
bombing and in 1954 it was rebuilt. In the early 1990s a
substantial redevelopment began to seat the North Bank in
accordance with the requirements of the Taylor report.
After the final game of the 1991–92 season the bulldozers
moved in and tore down the roof and much of the banking
to construct a new stand. In August 1993 the new North
Bank stand was opened. After some planning complaints
the local community was given a say in the design. The
result is a two-tier stand, magnificently developed in the
style of the old Highbury at a cost of £16.5 million.

NUTT, GORDON. Arsenal winger of the 1950s. Signed
from Cardiff City in September 1955 but was injured in
only his third match. He was out of action for more than
three months and after that found it hard to regain his
place on the left wing. His remaining time at Highbury
was mostly spent in the reserves, though he made the
occasional appearance in the first team. He left in 1960 to
join Southend United, having played 51 games.

O'FLANAGAN, KEVIN. One of the greatest all-round athletes ever to play for Arsenal. O'Flanagan was not only an Irish football international, but a rugby international as well. He was also Irish sprint champion in 1941, long jump champion four times, and, to top it all, was a doctor as well. O'Flanagan had played with the Irish club Bohemians prior to the Second World War and had won seven Irish caps. After the war he signed up with Arsenal as an amateur, making his debut in September 1946 against Blackburn Rovers. He went on to win a further three caps and was also capped as a rugby international. His duties as a doctor, however, meant that he was forced to miss many games, particularly away from home, and he made just 17 appearances for the club, scoring three goals. O'Flanagan could play in any forward position, though he was usually most comfortable as a centre-forward. He later played with Brentford before returning to Ireland to concentrate on his medical career. He was the Irish team doctor for three Olympic Games.

O'LEARY, DAVID. One of the most distinguished players in the club's history and the player who holds the all-time record for the number of appearances in an Arsenal shirt.

David O'Leary

Born in London, O'Leary's family returned to Dublin while he was still a toddler. He played as a junior with Shelbourne and made appearances for Ireland at schoolboy and youth level before coming to London to join Arsenal as an apprentice in June 1973. He made his league debut two years later at the beginning of the 1975–76 season against Burnley when he was only 17. He was to be virtually an ever-present in the heart of the Arsenal defence for the rest of his Highbury career, a career that would span almost 20 seasons. If he was absent, it was only because of injury. During his time he played in three FA Cup finals, the 1980 European Cup Winners Cup final and the Littlewoods Cup Final of 1987, and won two league championship medals with the Gunners. He was capped on more than 60 occasions by his country. O'Leary was a giant in the Arsenal defence, captain for many seasons, and was as reliable a defender as any in the Football League. He went on to make 558 league appearances for Arsenal. In 1993 he was surprisingly sold to Leeds United.

OLDEST INTERNATIONAL DEBUTANT. Arsenal's Leslie Compton was the oldest player ever to make his debut for any of the four home countries when he played for England against Wales in November 1950. He was aged 38 years and two months.

OLYMPICS. One Arsenal man who appeared in the Olympic Games was the famous amateur Bernard Joy. Joy not only played for the Great Britain side at the 1936 Olympic Games in Berlin but was also captain. In 1960 Laurie Brown, when he was with Bishop Auckland, played for Great Britain in the 1960 Rome Olympics. Another Arsenal Olympian was Stan Charlton, who played for Britain in the 1952 Helsinki games. At the time he was on the books of Leyton Orient as an amateur.

OVERSEAS PLAYERS. Over the years Arsenal have had a number of foreign players on their books. Among them have been: the Yugoslav international Vladimir Petrovic; Swedish internationals Anders Limpars and Stefan Schwartz; Siggi Jonsson from Iceland; Pal Lydersen from Norway; the Dane John Jensen and the Australian John Kosmina, who played for the club during the 1978–79 season.

P

PARKER, TOM. The first Arsenal man to lift the FA Cup. Parker was captain of Arsenal the day they first won the FA Cup, when they beat Huddersfield Town 2–0 at Wembley. Right-back Parker began his footballing days with Southampton, winning a Third Division South championship medal with them in 1922. He had an outstanding career with the south-coast side, helping them to an FA Cup semifinal in 1925 and winning an England cap in the same year. Unfortunately, it was the only cap he would win, despite many more years of distinguished service with the Gunners. He came to Highbury in March 1926, making his debut against Blackburn Rovers a month later. Over the next five seasons he would miss only two games. During his spell in the Arsenal defence, the Gunners went on to win not only the FA Cup but were runners-up in 1927 and in 1932 and league champions in 1931. Although Parker was on the slow side, his positional instinct more than made up for his lack of speed. He was a thoughtful defender, a strong tackler and an expert penalty-taker. In his 319 appearances he scored 22 goals, many of them from the spot. He quit Highbury in March 1933, exactly seven years after joining them, to become manager of Norwich. He later returned to his first club, Southampton, as manager.

Ray Parlour

PARLOUR, RAY. Joined Arsenal as a trainee in July 1989, turning professional in March 1991. An energetic midfielder, he was not expected to make the breakthrough for some time but as injuries struck, George Graham had little option but to throw him in at the deep end, giving him his debut against Liverpool at Anfield in January 1992. He began well but conceded a penalty in the second half as Arsenal went down 2–0. During the 1992–93 season he played 21 games for the club, appearing in the League Cup final and the FA Cup final, although he did not feature in the replay. Parlour is an England under-21 international.

PATERSON, JIMMY. Jimmy Paterson was not only a famous amateur footballer but a doctor, a First World War major and the holder of the Military Cross. Born in London, Paterson's family moved to Scotland while he was still young and he was brought up in Glasgow. He played as a professional with Glasgow Rangers, where he was known as an outstanding goalscoring winger. After qualifying as a doctor he played with Queens Park but on the outbreak of war enlisted with the London Scottish regiment as a medical officer. He was subsequently awarded the Military Cross while serving in France and rose to the rank of major. After the war he moved to London to join the practice of his brother-in-law, Dr J. L. Scott, who was also the Arsenal club doctor. It was not surprising that he soon joined Arsenal as an amateur and made his league debut for them in October 1920 against Derby County. He enjoyed three seasons playing with the Arsenal, making 81 appearances in total but scoring only three goals. Dr Paterson was well known for his impartiality. Referees doubtful about decisions often asked for his advice. In the true spirit of amateurism, his verdict frequently favoured the opposition. During the 1923–24 season he played for the South against the North. He had earlier been selected to play for the Football League against the Scottish League but injury had forced him to miss the game. He finally left Arsenal during the 1925–26 season to concentrate on his profession, thereby bringing to an end the footballing career of one of Arsenal's finest and most noted amateurs.

Vladimir Petrovic

PENALTY SHOOT-OUTS. Arsenal have been involved in a number of penalty shoot-outs but none will ever be quite as dramatic as that which brought an end to their European Cup Winners Cup dreams in 1980. After drawing 0–0 after extra time with Valencia in the final, the two teams then faced a penalty shoot-out to decide the winners. Sadly, Arsenal lost 4–5 with Graham Rix missing a vital spot kick. It was one of the most depressing occasions in the club's long history.

PETROVIC, VLADIMIR. Yugoslav international signed by Terry Neill from Red Star in December 1982. Petrovic was one of those frustrating players, a man you could never feel indifferent about. You either adored his breathtaking skills or loathed his inability to shrug off a tackle and get down to some hard work. Every time he played he demonstrated both sides of his game, one minute looping a perfect pass through the defence, the next being caught in possession or, worse still, standing around watching. He lasted just six months at Highbury, never acclimatising himself to the cut and thrust of English football, before being sold to Antwerp.

PITCH. The Arsenal pitch measures 110 × 71 yards.

PLUMSTEAD COMMON. Home of Arsenal from 1886 to 1887.

POWELL, JOE. Joe Powell is one of two players who have died as a result of playing for Arsenal. Playing for Royal Arsenal at Kettering in November 1896, Powell broke an arm and contracted tetanus. His arm had to be amputated but the tetanus continued to spread and he died six days later. Full-back Powell had been born in Bristol and played his early football with Walsall before joining Arsenal in 1892. He went on to play 201 games for the club and was a member of the side that played in Arsenal's first ever league game.

POWLING, RICHIE. Former England youth international

who made his debut in October 1973. He began life as a central defender but was converted, with some success, to the midfield. It would be a few more seasons, however, before he got an extended run in the side and even then he was never really in contention for a permanent spot. He finally quit the game in 1981 even though he was still young, having played just 54 games for the club.

PRICE, DAVID. Played in four FA Cup finals and the European Cup Winners Cup final but managed only one winners medal. That was in the 1979 FA Cup final against Manchester United, when Price excelled, creating a goal and giving a splendid performance. A former captain of England Schoolboys, Price was given his chance by Terry Neill during the early part of the 1977–78 season. He grabbed the opportunity and quickly became a permanent fixture in the Arsenal midfield, taking over from Trevor Ross. He held the position for the next couple of seasons until he was eventually squeezed out and then sold to Crystal Palace for £80,000. He was a useful midfielder, if not limited, but managed 164 games for the Gunners, scoring 19 goals. He ended his playing days with Leyton Orient.

PROGRAMME. The Arsenal programme has long been one of the most admired in the league. It has been produced regularly since the club was founded. In the early days it was a simple card with a list of fixtures and players. Under the editorship of George Allison, who was later to become manager of the side, it became a much more substantial production. During the 1930s it was a superb programme, copies of which are now collectors' items. After the war it took another step forward, with photographs inside and a colour cover in red, usually showing a photograph or drawing of Highbury. Since then it has developed even further to the rather more expensive, glossy, colour publication of today.

PROMOTION. Arsenal have been promoted on just one occasion. That was in 1903–4, when they finished second in division two and were duly promoted to the first division.

They were relegated in 1913 but were given an automatic place in the newly enlarged first division when football restarted after the First World War. Since then they have remained in the top division.

Q

QUICKEST GOAL. Timings are notoriously unreliable and we shall never know for certain the quickest goal ever scored by Arsenal, but among the principal contenders would be a goal scored by Alan Sunderland. It came in a League Cup replay against Liverpool at Villa Park in April 1980. Just four Arsenal players touched the ball with Sunderland scoring the goal in what is reckoned to have been less than ten seconds. No Liverpool player touched the ball.

QUINN, NIALL. At 6 feet 5 inches, Niall Quinn is almost certainly the tallest man ever at Highbury. The Irish striker came to Arsenal as a youngster, treading a well-worn path between Dublin and Highbury. He made his debut in December 1985 against Liverpool, giving the Liverpool central defenders, Hansen and Lawrenson, more than a few problems. He was ungainly and unpredictable but, as time wore on, he became more predictable. He was not always the best of goalscorers, though his runs and aerial power in the box presented many a goal to his colleagues. He scored a decisive goal against Tottenham in the 1987 League Cup semi-final that gave the Gunners a replay. Quinn subsequently appeared in the final and collected a winners medal. But there were no other honours for him during his Highbury career other than a bagful of international caps. He won his first Irish cap in 1986 and picked up a dozen while he was with Arsenal. In March 1990, not long after Alan Smith had been signed, Quinn decided that his chances of first-team football were becoming more limited and he opted for a move to Manchester City. He had played 81 games for Arsenal, scoring 20 goals.

R

RADFORD, JOHN. One of the greatest goalscorers in the history of the club. Radford was a Yorkshireman who joined Arsenal as an apprentice in October 1962, when the club was under the management of Billy Wright. It was Wright who was also to give him his first chance as he made his debut against West Ham in March 1964. But it was to be a few more years before he was able to claim a regular slot. Once he was in the side, however, he was there to stay, thanks mainly to Bertie Mee, who recognised his potential. Radford was strong in the air and just as deadly on the ground and it was largely thanks to his 23 goals during the 1970–71 season that Arsenal won the Double. Yet, although Radford was one of the most prolific goalscorers ever at Highbury, he never once hit more than 20 league goals in a season, sharing so many of the team's goals with Ray Kennedy, and only on four occasions did he strike a total of 20 or more in a season. His best season was undoubtedly the Double seasons and he ended his Highbury career with a grand total of 188 goals, just a few short of Cliff Bastin's record for the club – although Bastin's goals had come in just the league and Cup, whereas Radford also played in numerous other competitions. Among his many honours were a winners medal in the European Fairs Cup, a league championship medal, an FA Cup winners medal, plus various losers medals. Radford contributed to Arsenal's Fairs Cup victory with a goal in the second leg of the final, at Highbury. He also won four England under–23 caps and in January 1969 picked up the first of his two full England caps when he played against Romania. His second came two years later against Switzerland. Radford battled on as the darling of the North Bank until 1976, when the arrival of Malcolm Macdonald effectively ended his Highbury days. At the end of that year he moved to West Ham for £80,000, having played 542 games. He later had a spell with Blackburn Rovers.

RADIO. Arsenal played in the first football match to be broadcast on radio. The game took place on Saturday, 22 January 1927, when Arsenal faced Sheffield United at Highbury. A week earlier the BBC had broadcast the England v Wales rugby international from Twickenham. Three months later a further landmark in broadcasting history was reached when the Arsenal v Cardiff City FA Cup final was broadcast live from Wembley to homes all over the nation. One of the commentators on this occasion was George Allison, who would later become manager of the club.

RECORDS. Arsenal have beaten plenty of records over the years and have even made vinyl ones as well. The most memorable was undoubtedly 'Good Old Arsenal', made for the 1971 FA Cup final. Arsenal, however, were also the first club ever to make a record when they visited the Columbia recording studios a month before the 1932 FA Cup final. Arsenal featured on one side of the record, while their opponents Newcastle were on the other side.

REFEREE. Arsenal once had a manager who was also a qualified referee. He was George Morrell, manager of the club between 1908 and 1915.

RELEGATION. Arsenal have been relegated on just one occasion, from the first division to the second division. It was in 1913, when they finished 20th in the first division, having won just three of their 38 fixtures and ending the season with a mere 18 points. They returned to the top division two seasons later.

RICE, PAT. Rice was a Northern Ireland international even before he was a regular at Highbury. He made his debut for the club in December 1967, coming on as a substitute against Burnley, and won his first full cap the following year. But he did not command a regular spot in the side until the Double season, 1970–71. He had been born in Belfast but came to live in north London while he was still young. Inevitably, he was spotted by Arsenal and joined the club as a youngster in December 1964. He progressed through the various youth and reserve sides, even winning an FA Youth Cup winners medal in 1966. For ten seasons Rice was an automatic choice at right-back, winning league and Cup honours in 1971, another FA Cup winners medal in 1979, plus two FA Cup losers medals and a losers medal in the European Cup Winners Cup in 1980. He was also the club captain, winning 49 caps for his country, all while he was with Arsenal. Rice was a no-nonsense fullback. He was safe and sensible, not one given to trying anything foolish, and over the years proved to be one of the club's greatest servants, going on to make 588 appearances. In November 1980 he joined Watford, helping them to promotion into the first division. Then in July 1984 he returned to Highbury to coach the youth side, taking them to victory in the FA Youth Cup in 1988.

RICHARDSON, KEVIN. Richardson was already a League Championship medal winner with Everton before he wound up at Highbury. He arrived via Watford, costing George Graham a mere £200,000, and promptly went on to pick up a further championship medal. He did not remain long at Highbury, playing just 110 games, but it was long enough to prove that he was a player of genuine, if often underrated, quality. Richardson was a workhorse in the Gunners midfield – combative, determined, always leading by example. He may not have been the most skilful

Kevin Richardson

of players, but what he lacked he more than made up for
with his full-hearted approach. It was noticeable that once
he had left Goodison Everton went into decline. In the end
manager Graham and Richardson were at odds. There
could be only one winner, and Richardson was duly transferred to Real Sociedad for £750,000, giving Arsenal a more
than handsome profit. After leaving Spain, Richardson
returned to English football, joining Aston Villa and, much
to everyone's surprise, found himself being selected to play
for England against Greece in 1994, at the grand old age
of 31. It was more than deserved.

RIMMER, JIMMY. With a little luck Jimmy Rimmer could
have won European Cup winners medals with two different
clubs. As it was, he won just one. He was goalkeeper at
Old Trafford in 1968 but when it came to the European
Cup final he lost out on selection to Alex Stepney, and was
forced to sit on the bench. Then in 1982 with Aston Villa
he was injured in the European Cup final after just ten
minutes and had to leave the field, but at least he was able
to claim his medal. It was Bertie Mee who brought
Rimmer to Highbury, paying Manchester United £40,000
for him in February 1974. He then had three magnificent
seasons, playing 156 games for the club and proving to be
a valuable purchase. He even won an England cap but with
typical Rimmer luck never finished the game and never
played for his country again. That was the story of Rimmer.
In August 1977 Terry Neill signed Pat Jennings and the
same day Rimmer left for Aston Villa in a £70,000 deal.
But he was to enjoy a little more luck at Villa Park, winning
a championship medal, his European Cup medal and a
European Super Cup winners medal.

RIX, GRAHAM. Often underrated midfielder who contributed much to Arsenal's successes in the late 1970s and
1980s. A tall, gangly Yorkshireman, unmistakable with his
mop of curly hair, Rix worked effectively in the Gunners
midfield alongside Liam Brady. He joined the club as an
apprentice in 1974 and went on to play 446 games, scoring
51 goals. He played in three successive FA Cup finals, even

Graham Rix

providing the inch-perfect cross for Alan Sunderland to head home Arsenal's late winner against Manchester United in the 1979 final. A year later he was to miss a crucial penalty against Valencia in the European Cup Winners Cup final, a miss that is usually better remembered than any of his goals or assists. Perhaps his greatest handicap was in playing alongside Liam Brady, where obvious comparisons would be made. Rix's ability, however, did not go unrecognised outside Highbury. Ron Greenwood gave him his England opportunity in September 1980 against Norway and he was to play in the 1982 World Cup finals in Spain. At times he was even preferred to Hoddle. In all, he won 17 England caps, placing him among the elite of Arsenal's England men. That fact alone should be sufficient to guarantee him his spot in Arsenal's history. He was even captain of the club for a while until injury forced him to relinquish the role. His Arsenal career came to an end as new manager George Graham decided to give the club a good spring clean and Rix went off to France to join Caen.

ROBERTS, HERBERT. One of the first 'stoppers' in English football. Roberts took over the role from Jack Butler, who had been given the job by Herbert Chapman after the change in the offside law. But it was Roberts who really perfected the role. He was one of the stars of the great Arsenal side of the 1930s, joining the club from Oswestry Town for £200 in December 1926. Although he made his debut in April 1927, it was to be a couple of seasons before he eventually established himself as a regular. He then went on to make almost 350 appearances for Arsenal. During that time he won four league championship medals, an FA Cup winners medal, and two Charity Shield winners medals. On top of that he represented England, though winning only one cap, against Scotland in March 1931. England lost 2–0 that day, with the stopper role coming in for much criticism. In October 1937 he injured a knee playing against Middlesbrough and was forced to retire but he continued serving the club as trainer to the youth team. He died in June 1944 at the early age of 39.

ROBERTS, JOHN. Began his football with Swansea in the mid–1960s and then joined Northampton Town. Bertie Mee plucked him from the obscurity of Northampton in May 1969, bringing him to Highbury for £35,000. Roberts soon found a way into the team, beginning the 1970–71 Double season as regular choice. Midway through the season he lost his place to Peter Simpson, but he had done enough to earn himself a championship medal. The partnership of Simpson and McLintock, however, was far too strong for Roberts to prise apart and in October 1972 Birmingham City paid £115,000 for his services. But if Roberts had a problem getting into the Arsenal side, he certainly had little trouble with Wales, who capped him 22 times between 1971 and 1976, seven of those caps coming while he was with Arsenal. He made 77 appearances for the Gunners, scoring five goals. Roberts later had spells with Wrexham and Hull.

ROBERTSON, JIMMY. Joined Arsenal in October 1968 in a swap deal that took David Jenkins to White Hart Lane. Robertson, a useful if hardly spectacular winger, went on to play 58 games for the club. He had even won a Scottish cap during his Tottenham days but failed to add any honours to his name at Highbury. The signing of Peter Marinello brought an end to his Arsenal career and in March 1970 he joined Ipswich.

ROBSON, STEWART. Made his league debut at the age of 17 in December 1981 and looked set for a dazzling career. But, as so often happens, something went wrong *en route*. Robson had plenty of skill, as well as pace and aggression; something which was recognised by the England selectors, who gave him his first under-21 cap in 1984. Shortly after George Graham's arrival as new manager Robson was injured and took four months to recover. Then, just as he was set to reclaim his spot, he was off, joining West Ham, in a surprise £750,000 move. Robson had played 185 games for Arsenal and had looked set to be a fixture in the Gunners midfield for years. It left everyone wondering just what had happened. At Upton Park, however, his career never

David Rocastle

really took off as the Hammers battled against relegation. There were further injuries and in March 1991, after 80-odd games, he signed for Coventry City on a free transfer.

ROCASTLE, DAVID. Of the many youngsters who emerged through the Highbury youth scheme, David Rocastle was the one who caught the eye more than any other. He had a touch of class and arrogance about him. He was a beautiful passer of the ball and his imagination in the Arsenal midfield during a three-year spell that brought two championships was crucial to the team's success. He picked up his first medal in the Littlewoods Cup final victory over Liverpool in 1987, then two years later won his first championship medal. He won his first England call-up in September 1988 and would go on to win 14 caps while he was with the club. In 1991 he collected his second championship medal but by then his form was becoming erratic. His place, so secure in the preceding years, was now less certain. Injuries did not help either, and in July 1992 George Graham decided to cash in on his asset, selling him to the newly crowned league champions Leeds United for £2 million. Rocastle had played 218 league games for Arsenal, contributing 24 goals. Life at Elland Road, however, was little better as Leeds went into decline and Rocastle again found himself in and out of the side. In the spring of 1993 he left Leeds for Manchester City and the hope of regular first-team football.

ROOKE, RONNIE. One of the most extraordinary goal-scorers in the history of the club. Before the Second World War Rooke had been with Fulham and had a further two seasons with them after the war. During that time he had scored 77 goals in 110 games. In December 1946 he was sold to Arsenal, then languishing at the foot of the first division. It was an inspired signing. Over the next three seasons Rooke would score 83 goals in 102 games as Arsenal leapt from one end of the table to the other to clinch the title in 1948. He scored 41 goals in the championship season, 33 of them coming in the league. Had war not interrupted his career, Rooke would almost certainly have become one of the greatest goalscorers of all time. As it is, he tends to be forgotten when commentators talk about the great marksmen but his contribution at Highbury can never be overstated. Poor Rooke never even won an England cap nor any recognition by his country. But that was typical. Nobody ever regarded him as a quality centre-forward. With his bandy legs and flapping shirt he cut an almost amusing figure but the statistics tell a far different story. During the summer of 1949 he returned to Crystal Palace, the club where he had begun his footballing career, as player-manager.

ROPER, DON. Signed from Southampton in August 1947 by Tom Whittaker, Roper immediately went into the side that would clinch the title that season. In 1953 he added a second championship medal to his collection, which by then also included an FA Cup losers medal. Roper was a winger with a powerful shot, once hitting five goals in a floodlit friendly against Hibernian. But he could really play anywhere upfront, regularly switching wings, and in the 1952 Cup final he was forced into defence to take over from the injured Wally Barnes. In March 1953 he won an England B cap and also played for the Football League but never won full international honours. Roper played a total of 384 games for the club, scoring a creditable 134 goals. In the 1952–53 season he struck 21 goals, then 23 the following season and 22 the next. In January 1957 he left Highbury to rejoin Southampton.

ROSS, TREVOR. Made his league debut for Arsenal in February 1975 against Liverpool and went on to play 66 games for the club. Ross was a strong midfielder who liked to get forward. He had a powerful shot and plenty of pace but was never over-blessed with skill. Manager Terry Neill persisted with him until David Price arrived on the scene and then Ross was transferred to Everton for £170,000 in November 1977. Ross was an England schoolboy inter-national who had the unique distinction of then going on to play for Scotland Under–21.

ROYAL ARSENAL. Arsenal played under the name of Royal Arsenal between 1886 and 1891.

ROYALTY. On Saturday, 10 December 1932, HRH The Prince of Wales became the first member of the Royal Family to visit Highbury when he officially opened the new West Stand. It was extremely rare in those days for a member of the Royal Family to visit a football match other than the FA Cup final.

RUGBY. Kevin O'Flanagan, an Arsenal striker of the immediate post-war years, was also a rugby international. He won seven full caps playing football for Ireland just before the war, when he was a Bohemians player, and then a further three caps after the war, when he was with Arsenal. In that same post-war period he was also capped for Ireland at rugby.

RUMBELOWS CUP. See Football League Cup.

RUNNERS-UP. Arsenal have been first division runners-up on three occasions. When this is added to their ten championship titles it means that the club has finished in the top two in 13 of its 100 years in the Football League.

RUTHERFORD, JOCK. Even before he came to Arsenal, Rutherford was one of the most famous names in football. At Newcastle he had won three league championship medals, an FA Cup winners medal and four losers medals, as well as 11 England caps. He was 29 years old when Newcastle sold him to Arsenal in October 1913, no doubt thinking that he was near the end of his career, and with his receding hairline he certainly looked ten years older. But Rutherford was to play another nine seasons with the Gunners, finally retiring from football in 1927 after he had moved to Clapton Orient. It had been an extraordinary career. He played a total of 255 games for Arsenal, scoring 31 goals, and had even left the club at the end of the 1922–23 season to take over as manager of Stoke. But after a couple of months he resigned and returned to Arsenal, having barely missed a game. In his 11 games for England he was never on the losing side. His son was also an Arsenal player and they were on the club's books at the same time, but although they may have played some reserve matches together they never appeared in the same side at a senior level.

S

SAMMELS, JON. Sammels was for some years the unfortunate target of much abuse by the Highbury crowd, abuse which finally drove him out of the club. It was difficult to fathom why they should have targeted him. Arsenal were on the crest of a wave, winning the league and FA Cup, but for some reason Sammels came in for appalling abuse in every game. What made it all the sadder was that not only was Sammels an Arsenal man through and through but he was also a talented player. Like all players, he made mistakes but some fans seemed to pick him out for particular abuse. He was born in Ipswich but came to Highbury as a youngster, making his debut in April 1964. A couple of years later he succeeded George Eastham in the Gunners midfield and began to mature into a fine distributor of the ball. He was capped at England under–23 level and was a member of the 1970 European Fairs Cup winning side. Sammels missed the early part of the 1970–71 season with an ankle injury but recovered to reclaim his place, only to lose it again as the season wore on. But he had done enough to earn a championship medal. Unfortunately, he also missed out on the FA Cup final. By then the barracking of Sammels had reached disgraceful levels and was clearly beginning to affect his game. In the summer of 1971 he

decided that he had had enough and joined Leicester City
for £100,000. Arsenal were distressed to lose him and publicly blamed those on the terraces for his departure. At
Leicester he was to have a far happier time, playing more
than 200 games for the Midlands club.

SANDS, PERCY. Club captain for many years as a famous
amateur before he turned professional. Sands joined
Arsenal in December 1902 and was a prominent member
of the 1904 promotion-winning side. He was virtually a
permanent fixture in the Arsenal line-up from 1903 until
the outbreak of war, playing a total of 360 games for the
club. He played in two consecutive FA Cup semi-finals and
scored the winning goal in the Southern League Charity
Cup final in 1906. Sands was a school-teacher and when
he retired from football he went back into teaching. He
was never capped by England but did play in FA trials and
represented the Football League against the Irish League
in October 1905.

SANSOM, KENNY. The most capped player in the history
of the club, with 77 England caps to his name. Sansom had
already won nine caps before he joined Arsenal while he
was with Crystal Palace, giving him a career total of 86
caps. He came to Highbury in August 1980, one of Terry
Neill's most inspired signings, with Clive Allen, who had
never kicked a ball for the club, and goalkeeper Paul Barron
moving in the opposite direction. The cost was estimated
at £1 million. Sansom was an accomplished defender who
missed only a handful of games in his Highbury career but
at the end of his Arsenal days he had little to show in the
way of honours. He won a League Cup winners medal in
1987 and was on the losing side the following year but
apart from that, and of course his many England caps, he
had no other medals to boast. By the time George Graham
was putting together his title-winning side Sansom had left
to join Newcastle United. Graham had dropped him and
his Arsenal future was in doubt. By then his career was on
a downward spiral. He was 30 years old and his days at St
James's Park did not last long either as he made a fairly

Kenny Sansom

quick return to the capital to join Queens Park Rangers. But there is no doubt that Sansom will go down as one of the finest defenders in Arsenal's history, a full-back of composure, pace and elegance.

SATTERTHWAITE, CHARLIE. Satterthwaite had played for a number of clubs – including Liverpool, West Ham, Workington and Bury – before he wound up at Arsenal. He has the distinction of scoring Arsenal's first ever goal in the first division. An inside-forward, he went on to score 70 goals in 178 games for Arsenal between 1904 and 1910 before retiring. He played in an FA international trial but was never capped.

SCHWARZ, STEFAN. Swedish international signed by Arsenal from the Portuguese club Benfica for £1.5 million during the summer of 1994. Schwarz is a left-sided creative midfielder who played a major role in Sweden's 1994 World Cup side. Born in 1969 of a German father, he began his football career with Malmo. He almost signed for Bayern Munich some years ago but the deal collapsed when he refused to take up German nationality. He signed instead for Benfica. Schwarz also played in the 1990 World Cup finals and the 1992 European Championships.

SCORE – HIGHEST. Arsenal's highest score in any game was the 26–1 win over a Parisian XI in December 1904. The club's best ever victory in the Football League was the 12–0 win over Loughborough Town in a division two game in March 1900. Their biggest victory in the FA Cup is 11–1 against Darwen in January 1932. In February 1941, playing in the London War Cup, Arsenal beat Clapton Orient 15–2.

SCOTLAND. Arsenal have always had close links with Scottish football and over the years many famous Scottish internationals have played at Highbury. Among the most notable have been Alex James, Tommy Docherty, George Graham, David Herd, Jimmy Logie and Charlie Nicholas. The Scottish player who won most caps while at Highbury is Charlie Nicholas, who won 13 caps as a Gunner.

SCOTT, LAURIE. Laurie Scott's football for Arsenal spanned both sides of the Second World War but he did not make his league debut until after the war, in August 1946. He had joined the club as a youngster in February 1937 but with Male and Hapgood around there was little chance of him winning a place. During the war he played in two wartime Cup finals and won 16 wartime caps for England, and all this before he had played in a league game. But after the war he took up position as full-back, partnered by Wally Barnes, and went on to give splendid service. He was a member of the 1947–48 championship side, the 1950 FA Cup winning team and played 17 consecutive games for England. He won his first full cap in September 1946 as England thrashed Northern Ireland 7–2. His final cap came two years later against Wales, when he was injured. It was a particularly bad injury and, although he had two subsequent operations, Scott never fully recovered his old poise and authority. He played just 15 games the following season and after his second operation played another 17 the next season. Realising that he could not continue at the highest level, he left Arsenal in October 1951 to become player-manager of Crystal Palace.

SEAMAN, DAVID. The Yorkshire-born goalkeeper joined Arsenal from Queens Park Rangers in May 1990 for £1.3 million. Although George Graham had paid what was a record fee for a goalkeeper, as well as the biggest transfer deal Arsenal had ever concluded, he had managed to recoup £1 million with the sale of John Lukic to Leeds United. It made David Seaman, at £300,000, look like a bargain, especially as he was three years younger and a far better prospect. Ironically, Seaman had begun his footballing career with Leeds United but was given a free transfer when their second-string goalkeeper John Lukic began to perform so well. Seaman moved to Peterborough without ever having played a game for Leeds but soon got his chance at London Road. He then moved to Birmingham

City and wound up at Queens Park Rangers in a £225,000 deal. Meanwhile, Leeds had let Lukic go to Highbury for £75,000, only to have to buy him back for £1 million. It had been an expensive lesson for Leeds. Seaman went straight into the Arsenal side and was soon performing heroically. At the end of his first season he had picked up a championship medal. Then in 1993 he won a League Cup winners medal, followed by an FA Cup winners medal. The following year he was between the posts as Arsenal beat Parma to win the European Cup Winners Cup. Seaman won his first England cap in 1989 against Scotland while he was with QPR and was soon on his way to a dozen caps. A tall, athletic keeper, Seaman has two of the safest hands in the Premiership. Calm under pressure and highly respected, there is no better man to have in the last line of defence.

SECOND DIVISION. Arsenal have had just two spells in the second division. Their first began when the club came into league football in 1893 and lasted 11 seasons until 1904, when they finished second and were promoted. In 1913 they were relegated and returned to the second division. But their stay was to last for only two seasons. War interrupted and when it was over the first division was enlarged and Arsenal were given a place in the new first division.

SELLEY, IAN. Young Arsenal player who was just 18 years old when he played in the FA Cup semi-final at Wembley against Spurs. He did not, however, appear in the final, but a year later he did line up against Parma in the European Cup Winners Cup final, where he gave a solid performance to help Arsenal lift the trophy. He made his debut during the 1992–93 season and, although he still has only a few appearances to his name, he looks to have the potential to break through into the Arsenal first team very soon. Selley was an England youth international.

SEMI-FINALS. Up to the end of the 1993–94 season Arsenal had been involved in 18 FA Cup semi-finals.

SEXTON, DAVE. Coach at Arsenal under Bertie Mee for a brief time. As a player, he had been with Luton and West Ham United. After coaching at Highbury he had a highly successful spell as manager of Chelsea before managing, among others, QPR, Manchester United and Coventry. Sexton currently coaches the England under-21 team.

SHARP, JIMMY. Scottish international full-back who played for Arsenal between 1905 and 1908. He began his career with Dundee, where he won his first Scottish cap, then moved to Fulham but after just a season with them joined Woolwich Arsenal in June 1905. A strong, resourceful full-back, he played in the club's two consecutive Cup semi-finals but had little else to show for his endeavours, though he did win three more Scottish caps. With the club sinking further into financial difficulties, Sharp was one of many players offloaded, sold to Glasgow Rangers for £400. He later returned to his former club Fulham and also had a spell with Chelsea.

SIMPSON, PETER. Simpson was as tough a defender as you could imagine. Little got past him. He was calm, committed and, above all, was a footballing defender, the kind of player every team longs for. He joined Arsenal in May 1960 as a 15-year-old, making his debut in March 1964 against Chelsea. It was not a particularly good start. Simpson was given the task of marking Bobby Tambling that day – Tambling scored all four Chelsea goals as the Pensioners cruised to a comfortable victory at Highbury. But manager Billy Wright was not too worried, though it was not until the arrival of Bertie Mee a couple of seasons later that Simpson began to establish himself as a regular first-team player. Over 15 seasons Simpson gave admirable service, playing 534 games. During that time he won losers medals in the 1968 and 1969 League Cup finals, picked up a winners medal in the 1970 Fairs Cup triumph, then league and Cup winners medals in 1971, and finally losers medals in the 1972 and 1975 FA Cup finals. Eventually, his tough-tackling, take-no-prisoners attitude began to take its toll. Injuries crept up on him and he began to find himself on the touchlines more often than in the side. In April 1978 he decided to move on, joining the exodus to America to join the New England Teamen. Yet, despite his distinguished career at Highbury, it was astonishing that Simpson was never capped by his country. He did make the squad of 22 for the 1970 World Cup finals but was never chosen to play. Perhaps the presence of Norman Hunter and Bobby Moore, two of the most formidable and elegant central defenders in world football, was more than a match even for Peter Simpson.

SKIRTON, ALAN. The most expensive non-league footballer when he signed for Arsenal for £5,000 from Bath City. But even before he had pulled on a first-team shirt he was out of action with illness for a year-and-a-half. Eventually, he recovered sufficiently to make his debut during the 1960–61 season. He went on to play 153 games for the club, usually on the wing, where his remarkable speed brought a touch of excitement to the Highbury terraces. Skirton was so powerful and strong that once he started off down the flanks it took a courageous full-back to stand in his way. In 1966 Skirton, much to the surprise of the club and fans, opted for a transfer to Blackpool, who paid £65,000 for him.

SMALLEST PLAYER. Although such statistics are always unreliable and were generally not even available for those playing before 1900, the distinction of being Arsenal's smallest player probably belongs to Joe Haverty who was just 5 feet 3 inches. Not surprisingly, Haverty was a winger who played during the 1950s.

SMITH, ALAN. Smith was an expensive signing who has not always been the automatic choice upfront. He came from Leicester City in March 1987 for £800,000, already a highly rated goalscorer who had enjoyed a productive partnership at Filbert Street with Gary Lineker. Smith began his Highbury days in competition with Niall Quinn, a battle he regularly lost. But in the championship season 1988–89 he began to deliver the goals, topping the first division scoring list with 23. He was now first choice but the following season seemed to lose his sharpness, scoring less frequently, just ten, perhaps missing the crosses of Brian Marwood. In his second championship season the goals came more easily, 27 this time, but shortly after that Ian Wright arrived to challenge for his spot. Kevin Campbell was also a contender and Smith frequently found himself sidelined by the pair. Smith missed out in the 1993 League Cup final but did make it for the FA Cup final, coming on as a substitute in the first game. In the replay he was there in his own right. With Ian Wright ineligible for the European Cup Winners Cup final, Alan Smith won his place and, with a magnificent performance as the lone man upfront, kept the Parma defence more than occupied for the entire evening, scoring the only goal of the match. Smith won his first England cap in 1989 against Scotland and has now collected more than a dozen honours for his country.

SMITH, LIONEL. Post-war full-back who stepped into the slot vacated by the injured Laurie Scott and went on to form a formidable partnership with Wally Barnes. Smith had joined the club immediately before the war but had to wait until May 1948 to make his league debut, just after Arsenal had clinched the league title. But he did manage to win a championship medal with the 1952–53 side, though he missed out on an FA Cup medal in 1950. In 1952 he won a runners-up medal as Arsenal lost to Newcastle in the Cup final. By then he was also an England international, having won the first of his six caps against Wales in November 1950. His final cap came in the 2–2 draw with Scotland in April 1953. Smith also played three times for the Football League. He left Arsenal in June 1954 to join Watford, having played 205 games for the Gunners.

SNEDDEN, JOHN. Made his debut as a 17-year-old against Tottenham in January 1960. He began the following season as first choice in the centre-half spot but at the end of the year was seriously injured, breaking an ankle against Sheffield Wednesday. That put him out of action for the rest of the season but he returned as the new season started to reclaim the number 5 jersey. But his form had deteriorated and he soon found himself sidelined. Manager Billy Wright tried him at wing-half briefly, with some success, but injury struck again and that was virtually the end of his Arsenal career. In 1965 he moved to Charlton Athletic for £15,000 but the sure, confident touch of his teenage days never returned and he was soon on his way to Orient.

SPONSORS. Arsenal were one of the first clubs in the Football League to have sponsors and have stayed with their original sponsors, JVC since 1979.

SPORTSMAN GROUND. Home of Arsenal from 1887 to 1888.

STAPLETON, FRANK. The Dublin-born striker was originally on the books of Manchester United but was allowed to leave without ever having played a game for them. He was still young and ended up with Arsenal, signing on as an apprentice in June 1972. He made his league debut in March 1975 and soon formed an impressive partnership with Malcolm Macdonald. Stapleton was a powerful striker, full of running, a superb header of the ball and with a strong shot. He was always a difficult man to knock off the ball and in 334 games for the Gunners hit 125 goals. He won his first cap for the Republic of Ireland in October 1976 and won 24 caps while he was an Arsenal player. During his Highbury days he played in three consecutive FA Cup finals and a European Cup Winners Cup final but came out of all that with only one winners medal. But it was his header in the 1979 final which helped Arsenal to the Cup. He had already netted five times on the way to Wembley. It was his best season for Arsenal, with a total of 30 goals. In the summer of 1981 his contract came to an end and, failing to agree terms with Arsenal, he was transferred to Manchester United. The fee, later agreed at a tribunal, was just under £1 million, far less than Arsenal had been asking. The whole deal left Arsenal fans bitter and angry, feeling that the popular Stapleton ought never to have been allowed to leave the club. At Old Trafford he won further honours, picked up more Irish caps and then moved to Ajax of Amsterdam. He later had spells with Derby County, Le Havre and Blackburn Rovers.

STORER, HARRY. Arsenal goalkeeper who was also the first player at the club to gain major representative honours when he was selected to play for the Football League against the Scottish League in April 1895. Storer was born in Derbyshire and played with Derby County, Gainsborough Trinity and Loughborough Town before linking up with Arsenal in May 1894. He made 40 appearances for the club but was then suspended following a breach of discipline. Not long after that he left, joining Liverpool and helping them to the second division championship and to become runners-up in the first division. Storer also played county cricket for Derbyshire.

STOREY, PETER. During the late 1960s and the 1970s Arsenal boasted some of the toughest defenders in football. Among them was Peter Storey, who began his career as a full-back but in later years moved into the midfield to become Arsenal's principal ball-winner. He joined the club as a youngster in 1962 after winning England schoolboy honours. He made his league debut against Leicester City in October 1965 and went on to play 571 games for the Gunners. He played in the 1968 and 1969 League Cup finals and then picked up a winners medal in the 1970 European Fairs Cup as well as league and FA Cup winners honours a year later. In 1972 he picked up a losers medal in the FA Cup final against Leeds United. Storey also won 19 England caps, his first coming in April 1971 against Greece. In 1976 he found himself left out of the side. He eventually grew weary of reserve football and in March 1977 moved to Fulham for £100,000. He played just 17 league games for them before drifting out of football. Storey would later hit the headlines again, though not for reasons he would want to be remembered for, as he found himself in trouble with the law.

STRONG, GEOFF. Joined Arsenal in September 1957 but did not make his debut until three years later. After a couple of seasons on the fringes he finally made the breakthrough into regular first-team football in 1962. Strong epitomised his name. He had a powerful shot, plenty of skill and was committed. With Joe Baker or George Eastham alongside him, he was capable of scoring goals as well as creating them. In the 137 games he played for Arsenal, Strong scored a remarkable 77 goals – not bad for someone never considered as an out-and-out goalscorer. Then, much to everyone's surprise, manager Billy Wright sold him to Liverpool in November 1964 for £40,000. His strength was that he could play almost anywhere and at Liverpool became something of a utility player, winning a bagful of medals. Liverpool's gain had undoubtedly been Arsenal's loss.

SUBSTITUTES. The first ever Arsenal substitute was Alan Skirton, who came on for John Sammels on 28 September 1965 in the 1–1 draw with Northampton Town.

SUNDERLAND, ALAN. Began life as a midfielder with Wolves and was transferred to Arsenal in November 1977 for £240,000. In 1974 he had won a League Cup winners medal with Wolves and had been capped at under-21 and under–23 levels. At Highbury he immediately took up residence in the Gunners midfield but when Malcolm Macdonald was injured Sunderland was pushed up front, alongside Frank Stapleton. He was a revelation, quick and strong, and he and Stapleton formed as dangerous a pair of strikers as any in the division. During the 1979–80 season he struck 30 goals, six of those coming in the FA Cup. He played in all three FA Cup finals of the period and was the man who won the cup for Arsenal in 1979 with his late strike against Manchester United, a goal that was to guarantee him a place in the hearts of Gunners fans forever. The curly-haired Sunderland went on to play 317 games for the club, scoring 101 goals. He also added to his England honours with a full international cap against Australia in May 1980 but was substituted and never played again. The arrival of Tony Woodcock and then Charlie Nicholas signalled the end of his Highbury days. He was dropped during the 1983–84 season and in the summer of 1984 he was given a free transfer to Ipswich Town. Sunderland scored one of the quickest goals ever in the history of Arsenal when he put the ball in the net after just a few seconds in a League Cup replay against Liverpool in April 1980.

SWINDIN, GEORGE. Arsenal goalkeeper and manager. Yorkshire-born Swindin began his league career with Bradford City in 1934 but after just 26 appearances spanning two seasons he was transferred to Arsenal for £4,000. He made his debut against Brentford in September 1936 and the following season picked up a championship medal. War then intervened but he was still young enough to reappear in his familiar spot between the posts after hostilities. He won a second championship medal in 1948, an FA Cup winners medal in 1950, a losers medal in 1952 and then a third league championship medal in 1953. In February 1954 he was given a free transfer, allowing him to become player-manager of Peterborough United. He had been at Highbury for 18 years and there is little doubt that had war not interrupted his career then Swindin would have clocked up even more honours as well as hundreds more games. As it was, he made 350 appearances for the Gunners. He was never capped by England, as he was unfortunate enough to be vying for the goalkeeper's spot at the same time as Frank Swift and, later, Bert Williams, though he was twice named as a substitute. At Peterborough Swindin turned out to be a more than useful manager, taking the club to three successive Midland League championships. Then, in 1958, he was invited to return to Highbury to take over the managerial chair. He began with a massive spring-clean, signing Tommy Docherty, Billy McCullough, Jackie Henderson and others, while Derek Tapscott, Stan Charlton, Cliff Holton and a few more were shown the door. It seemed to do the trick, with Arsenal finishing in third spot after looking like they might take the title. Injuries and a poor run at the end of the season had cost the Gunners the championship. They began the next season among the favourites but further injuries wreaked havoc and they finished in 13th place. The changes continued, with more players joining and others leaving. Meanwhile, Spurs were riding the crest of a wave and Arsenal fans were hardly thrilled. The pressures on Swindin mounted and in the summer of 1962 he resigned. He had been desperately unlucky, forced to bring in new players as others became injured and never really able to find a settled side. There had been far too many changes. But while Swindin's managerial career at Highbury may not linger too long in the memory, the same can never be said of his goalkeeping career and he will always be remembered as one of the finest goalkeepers Arsenal ever boasted.

T

TALBOT, BRIAN. Signed from Ipswich in January 1979 for a club record fee of £450,000 and went on to play more than 360 games for the club over the next six years. Born in Ipswich, Talbot began his playing career with his local club, making his league debut in February 1974. Two years later he was an England under–23 international and on his way to full England honours. He won the first of his six England caps in May 1977 against Northern Ireland but only one of those caps came while he was an Arsenal player. He also won six England B caps while he was at Ipswich. In 1978 he appeared in a Wembley Cup final as Ipswich beat the Gunners 1–0. So impressed was Terry Neill by his display that day that seven months later he signed him. Talbot then went on to appear in the final the following year, and was again on the winning side as Arsenal beat Manchester United 3–2. It made him the first player to ever pick up winners medals in consecutive finals with different clubs. As if that was not enough, he then re-appeared at Wembley the following season but this time he was on the losing side as the Gunners went down 1–0 to West Ham. Talbot was a tenacious midfielder, always willing to run and tackle, even for lost causes, but combined his commitment with undeniable skill. During the 1985 close season Watford paid £150,000 for him but by then he had seen his best days. He later had spells with West Bromwich Albion, Fulham and Aldershot before taking over as manager at the Hawthorns.

TALLEST PLAYER. It is impossible to say for certain who has been the tallest player ever on Arsenal's books as such records are always unreliable. But Niall Quinn, at 6 feet 5 inches, is probably the chief contender for the prize. Of the current squad, David Seaman, Steve Bould, and Andy Linighan all stand at 6 feet 4 inches. Another 6 feet 4 inches man was Jim Fotheringham, a defender of the 1950s.

TAPSCOTT, DEREK. Signed from amateurs Barry Town in October 1953 for £2,750. Tapscott made his league debut against Liverpool a year later but it was to be a day of mixed fortunes. Tapscott performed well but the occasion was marred by an injury to Joe Mercer that ended his career. But Tapscott went on to play more than 150 games for the Gunners, scoring almost 100 goals for the club. It was an impressive strike rate, considering that he never really regarded himself as an out-and-out goalscorer. He was really an inside-forward, creating goals for the likes of David Herd. He was the club's leading goalscorer in consecutive seasons, with 25 league goals during the 1956–57 campaign, his best season, and a grand total of 41. He won his first Welsh cap, against Austria in Vienna, in May 1954 and won a further 11 caps as a Gunner. In all, he would be capped 14 times by his country but missed out on the 1958 World Cup finals. Just when he was at his peak, in 1957, he received a serious injury and lost much of the sparkle that had made him such a quick and dangerous striker. In September 1958 he was transferred to Cardiff City for £10,000, a move that briefly resurrected his career. The goals returned, though never in such an abundance as they had at Highbury but he was still able to hit 79 in 194 appearances. He was also capped again by Wales. He left Cardiff in 1965, joining Newport County. Tapscott was a much underestimated player who might well have gone on

to become one of the great Arsenal goalscorers had injury
not dealt him so cruel a blow.

TELEVISION. Highbury was the venue for the first ever
televised football match anywhere in the world when on 16
September 1937 Arsenal played their own reserves. Extracts
from the game were shown on television that afternoon.
The day before there had been a technical rehearsal but
that was never shown publicly. The main reason why Highbury was chosen was its close proximity to Alexandra
Palace, where BBC television was based. Arsenal were also
involved in the first ever *Match of the Day* programme on
22 August 1964, when they played Liverpool at Anfield.
The game was shown that evening on BBC2 with a national
audience of 75,000, not that many more than the 47,000
who watched inside Anfield. A black cat appeared on the
pitch that day and chased around the Kop goal before
disappearing into the crowd. It was to prove a lucky omen
for the BBC's new programme, which 30 years later is still
going strong.

TESTIMONIALS. Although the club has given testimonials
to many players in its history, perhaps the most successful
was George Armstrong's in March 1974 when just over
36,000 turned up to see Arsenal play Barcelona.

THOMAS, MICHAEL. Michael Thomas will always be
remembered by Arsenal fans for one thing: his last-gasp
goal in 1989 against Liverpool at Anfield that clinched the
league championship for the Gunners. Latching on to a
flick from Alan Smith, Thomas powered into the Liverpool
penalty area and slotted a superb drive past Bruce Grobbelaar. Thomas joined Arsenal as a youngster but made his
league debut while he was on loan to Portsmouth. Then
in February 1987 he was called upon to deputise for the
injured Viv Anderson. Some of his early games for the Gunners were at right-back and it was not until later in the
1987–88 season that he was shifted into a central-midfield
role. From there he went on to bring a dash of excitement
and more than a few goals to Arsenal as he powered at

defenders. A former captain of England schoolboys, youth and under-21s, he won his first full England cap under Bobby Robson in 1989. For a while he lost his way at Highbury but form eventually returned. Then in November 1991 he was surprisingly sold to Liverpool, of all clubs, for £1.5 million. At Arsenal he won league championship honours in 1989 and 1991 and played against Liverpool in the 1987 League Cup triumph at Wembley. At Anfield he added an FA Cup winners medal to his collection in 1992 but injury disrupted his playing career and robbed him of most of the next season and a half. Thomas was capped twice by England while he was at Arsenal. He made 163 league appearances for the Gunners, scoring 24 goals – none ever more crucial than the one he scored that night at Anfield.

TITANIC DISASTER FUND. One of the more unusual charity games Arsenal ever took part in was played in April 1912, when they played Tottenham Hotspur at the White City for the Titanic Disaster Fund. Arsenal won 3–0.

TOURS. Arsenal were one of the first clubs ever to undertake close-season tours. Their first such adventure was in May 1906, when they visited Belgium, Holland, Germany, Czechoslovakia, Austria and Hungary. Their first game was against a Belgian XI, which they won 2–1. They ended their tour with seven victories and one draw and 43 goals scored. During the 1930s, they were frequent visitors to France, with regular annual games against Racing Club de Paris. In May 1949 they undertook the most extensive tour in their history when they visited Brazil, where they notched up victories against Fluminese and Corinthians, but were defeated by Vasco da Gama, Flamengo and Sao Paulo. The following year they returned to Brazil, only to lose five out of their six fixtures. But perhaps the club's most famous tour came in October 1955, when they became the first British club to visit the Soviet Union. It was also a memorable occasion because Arsenal were thrashed 5–0 by Moscow Dynamo in front of 90,000. Since then Arsenal, one of the most popular clubs in world football, have continued to tour the world, playing in places as far afield as South Africa, the West Indies, Cyprus, Israel, Japan, Malaysia, Turkey, Kuwait, Australia, Egypt and Indonesia.

TRAGEDY. During the First World War the Arsenal full-back Bob Benson collapsed and died while playing for the club. Benson had not played football for a year but had gone to watch Arsenal playing Reading at Highbury. Arsenal were a man short and Benson volunteered to play. During the game, however, he was taken ill and had to come off. Later, in the dressing-room, he collapsed and died. There had earlier been another tragedy for an Arsenal player when in November 1896 Joe Powell broke an arm while playing for the club. Unfortunately, Powell also contracted blood poisoning and tetanus and the arm had to be amputated. But the blood poisoning continued to spread and six days later Powell died at his home in Plumstead.

TRANSFERS, RECORD. Arsenal have broken the British transfer record on a number of occasions and were the first club to break the £10,000 barrier when Herbert Chapman signed David Jack from Bolton Wanderers for £10,980. They broke the British transfer record a few years later when they paid Wolverhampton Wanderers £14,000 for Bryn Jones. More recently the club record has been broken by Malcolm Macdonald, who was signed from Newcastle for £333,000 in 1976, David Seaman, who came to Arsenal from QPR in May 1990 for £1.3 million, and Ian Wright, signed from Crystal Palace in September 1991 for £2.5 million.

TUBE STATION. In 1932 the Arsenal manager, Herbert Chapman, spent weeks negotiating with the London Passenger Transport Board in order to persuade them to change the name of Gillespie Road tube station. He was successful and from 5 November 1932 the station formally became known as Arsenal.

TURNBULL, BOB. Scottish-born full-back who joined Arsenal as an amateur in January 1921, turning professional later that year. Much of his early career was spent in reserve-team football, although he made his league debut in December 1921 against Cardiff City as a full-back. But it was not until the 1922–23 season, when he was converted to centre-forward, that he really began to shine. That season Turnbull hit 20 league goals in 35 games and scored a grand total of 35 goals in 48 matches over the season – enough to pull the Gunners out of the relegation zone and into mid-table respectability. Over the Christmas period he struck ten goals in four games, including four goals against Bolton and another four against Blackburn Rovers. But after that season his Highbury career took a nose-dive. Defenders began to get the better of him, and the following season he scored just six league goals and began to drift out of the side. He was eventually transferred to Charlton Athletic in November 1924 but only stayed a short time before joining Chelsea, where some of his old goalscoring ability returned as he notched up 29 goals in 26 appearances. He later played with Clapton Orient, Southend and Crystal Palace, where he was also trainer.

U

UEFA CUP. Formerly known as the Inter-Cities Fairs Cup. Arsenal first participated in 1963, defeating Staevnet of Denmark 7–1 away in their opening game but losing 3–2 at Highbury. In the next round they lost 4–2 on aggregate to Standard Liege. The next time they competed, in 1969, the name of the competition had been changed to the European Fairs Cup. This time Arsenal went on to win the trophy, beating Anderlecht 4–3 on aggregate in the final. As winners, they then competed the following year but were knocked out by Cologne in the quarter-finals, losing on the away-goal rule. By the time they next competed, in 1978, the competition's name had been changed yet again, this time to the UEFA Cup. That season they reached the third round before being knocked out by Red Star Belgrade. During the 1981–82 season they reached the third round, before losing to Winterslag of Belgium, again on the away-goal rule. The following season they went out in the opening round, losing to Moscow Spartak 8–4 on aggregate.

UNDEFEATED. Arsenal have never gone a season undefeated.

UNDEFEATED – AT HOME. Arsenal have gone just four seasons undefeated at home. They were 1903–4, 1970–71, 1980–81 and 1990–91.

UNIVERSITY. Arsenal have had a number of university graduates over the years. The most notable was probably Dr Jimmy Paterson.

URE, IAN. Popular Scottish centre-half of the 1960s. Born in Ayr, he began his professional career with Dundee, where he won international honours, a Scottish league championship medal and helped Dundee into a European Cup semi-final. In August 1963 he moved to Arsenal in a £62,500 deal that was a record for a centre-half, hoping that it might bring even further honours. Unfortunately, it did not bring him very much reward. In his first game Arsenal were beaten 1–3 at Highbury by Wolves, with Ure something of a bystander. For some time it looked as if Ure had been a disastrous mistake but gradually he settled down. He made just three more appearances for Scotland and was on the losing side in two League Cup finals. But he was always popular. Tall, robust, a fine header of the ball, he was a towering figure in the Gunners defence. On the ground, however, he was not quite so adept, often looking flat footed and slow. He was also a controversial character, sent off four times in his Arsenal career, including a famous dismissal with Denis Law. He went on to play almost 300 games for the club, but with his first-team place in question he moved to Manchester United in August 1969 for £80,000. He later played with St Mirren.

V

VAESSEN, PAUL. Paul Vaessen made his Arsenal debut when he was 18 years old, coming on as a substitute to score a last-minute goal against Juventus in the semi-final of the European Cup Winners Cup that sent Arsenal into the final. All seemed set for a glittering career but then in late 1980 he injured a knee and not long after was forced to quit the game. It was an appalling tragedy, especially given his age and promise. He had played just 27 games and had scored nine goals.

VICTORY INTERNATIONALS. A number of Arsenal players represented their country during the Victory and wartime internationals. The most notable were the two Compton brothers, Leslie and Denis, Alf Kirchen, Laurie Scott and Eddie Hapgood.

VIDEOS. Arsenal have produced a number of videos in conjunction with the BBC, the most notable being an official history of the club.

WALFORD, STEVE. Joined Arsenal from Tottenham Hotspur in August 1977 for £25,000. He had been bought as a successor to Peter Simpson in the centre of the Gunners defence but, while he showed promise, in the end he never delivered. He made his debut in September 1977 and went on to play 77 games for the club. He won an FA Cup winners medal in 1979, coming on as a substitute for David Price, but that was just about the limit of his success. In March 1981 he was sold to Norwich and later had a more successful spell with West Ham United.

WAR. During the Second World War no less than nine players on the Arsenal staff died. It was the highest loss of any club. The nine were Henry Cook, Bobby Daniel, William Dean, Hugh Glass, Leslie Lack, William Parr, Sidney Pugh, Herbie Roberts and Cyril Tooze.

WAR DECORATIONS. A number of Arsenal players were decorated for bravery during the First World War. The most notable was Major Jimmy Paterson, who was awarded the Military Cross while serving in France. Paterson, who was a doctor, was Medical Officer of the London Scottish regiment. During the First World War Billy Milne, who was a sergeant with the Seaforth Highlanders, was awarded the DCM in 1918 for gallantry in France. Milne, however, did not join Arsenal until after the war. Charlie Buchan also won the Military Medal during the First World War, although at the time he was on Sunderland's books and did not come to Arsenal until many years later.

WAR FOOTBALL. Arsenal, like most clubs, continued to play football during both wars, even though the normal Football League programme had been suspended. During the First World War they played in the London Combination. This was a grouping of London clubs and a few other southern clubs. Arsenal did not win any honours during this period, although they finished as runners-up to Brentford in the 1918–19 season. During the Second World War the Football League was again suspended. Arsenal, however, continued to play in various leagues which were again formed around the London and southern clubs. In their first season they were champions of the League South A Division and in their second season reached the Football League War Cup, only to lose the replayed final 1–2 to Preston North End. In 1941–42 they were champions of the London League and semi-finalists in the London War Cup. The following season they topped the Football League South and won the Football League South Cup, beating Charlton Athletic 7–1 in the final at Wembley. Unfortunately, that was to be their final honour as they performed only moderately well throughout the remainder of the war. There were also some staggering scorelines during the war, with Arsenal beating Clapton Orient 15–2 in the London War Cup. Leslie Compton scored ten goals that day. Millwall were also beaten 10–0 on one occasion. As with most clubs during this period, Arsenal fielded guest players, among them Stanley Matthews, Stan Mortensen and Bill Shankly. Highbury stadium was closed during the war and was used as a major Air Raid Precautions centre, with Arsenal forced to play all their home games at neighbouring White Hart Lane.

WARD, GERRY. The youngest ever player to pull on the

Arsenal colours, when, as a 16-year-old, he made his debut against Huddersfield Town in August 1953. He played so well that he was hailed as the next 'Boy' Bastin and was chosen for the next two games. He was then dropped and never reappeared until five years later, in February 1958, when he faced Manchester United just a few days before their ill-fated trip to Yugoslavia. After that, Ward began to get more regular call-ups but was never really an automatic choice. Somehow he was always fighting for his place, always trying to convince. In the end there was too much choice at Highbury, with Tommy Docherty, Mel Charles and Vic Groves competing with Ward for a place in the midfield. In 1963, after 84 games he moved on, joining Leyton Orient.

WEMBLEY. Arsenal have made many appearances at Wembley, though it was not until April 1927 that they first appeared there, when they lost 0–1 to Cardiff City in the Cup final. In all, they have made 13 Wembley appearances in FA Cup finals (including a replay), five appearances in the Football League Cup final and two appearances in the wartime Cup. They have also played there in minor close season tournaments, in two FA Cup semi-finals and in four Charity Shield games.

WHITTAKER, TOM. Arsenal manager from 1947 to 1956. Whittaker joined Arsenal in November 1919 and went on to play 70 games for the club, many of them during the war, when he also won two London FA Challenge Cup winners medals. In 1925, as the club toured Australia, Whittaker was injured and was forced into early retirement. The following year he was appointed assistant trainer, succeeding George Hardy as trainer less than 12 months later. With Herbert Chapman at the helm, Arsenal went on to achieve worldwide fame and Whittaker more than played his part in that success. He was also appointed trainer to the England side, an even more important position then than it is today. After the Second World War Arsenal made Whittaker into manager George Allison's assistant and when Allison retired in May 1947 Whittaker was the obvi-

Tom Whittaker

ous successor. By the end of his first season in charge Arsenal had won the league title. Two years later they added the FA Cup to their honours and then in 1953 clinched the title for a second time. In between, Arsenal had made another Wembley appearance in the FA Cup, this time losing to Newcastle. It had been an outstanding period but the Arsenal side was now ageing. A major rebuilding of the team was needed. There followed a couple of years in the doldrums as Whittaker worked to find new players and the correct blend of youth and experience. But it was not easy and the effort took its toll on his health. In 1956 he was ordered to rest but it was too late. He eventually entered hospital suffering from nervous exhaustion, and a short time later, in October of that year, died of a heart-attack. Whittaker was undoubtedly one of the greatest servants the club has ever had, spending 37 years with them. In his time they won countless honours and a reputation that has lived on to this day. Whittaker was also awarded the MBE for his services to football.

WHYTE, CHRIS. Yet another north London boy who

matured through the ranks at Highbury. He made his debut in October 1981 and held on to his place for the next 15 months. During that time he won England under-21 honours and looked to be settled for a long and distinguished career at the club. But sadly his form deteriorated and, with other central defenders knocking on the door, he was given a free transfer in 1986. He was distraught and went off to America but returned to revive his career with West Bromwich Albion. Leeds United spotted his return to form and snapped him up in 1990. He has since gone on to win a league championship medal with Leeds, demonstrating that perhaps Arsenal were a little hasty in letting him go, particularly on a free transfer. He played 105 games for Arsenal.

WILLIAMS, STEVE. A Don Howe signing in December 1984 when Howe paid Southampton £500,000. Williams began well at Highbury, his precision passing a huge bonus for the developing Arsenal side. But once George Graham was ensconced in the managerial chair his form deteriorated. Graham did not seem to rate his ability as highly as others and after a while he found himself sidelined by the new manager. But he did win a League Cup winners medal in the victory over Liverpool in 1987 and was capped six times by England between 1983 and 1985. But after Graham had dropped him for the League Cup final against Luton Town, he decided that his future lay elsewhere. In July 1988 he was, ironically, transferred to Luton Town for £300,000. Williams had been a player who had promised much but in the end had not quite delivered.

WILLS, LEN. Full-back of the 1950s. Wills was a one-club man, joining Arsenal in the early 1950s. He made his debut in 1953, making an immediate impression. By the mid-50s, however, he had been usurped by Stan Charlton but fought back to regain his place later in the decade. He made 208 appearances for the Gunners and, although he was never regarded as a tenacious defender, he was a fine passer of the ball and had plenty of pace. He retired at the end of the 1960–61 season.

Bob Wilson

WILSON, BOB. Arsenal goalkeeper of the Double side. Wilson was born in Chesterfield, the home of so many outstanding goalkeepers, including Sam Hardy, Ray Clemence and later John Lukic. Although he played for England Schoolboys, Wilson never imagined that he would ever have a career in football and opted instead to train as a PE teacher at Loughborough College. He was officially on Wolves's books but eventually found himself joining Arsenal in July 1963. He made his league debut later that year while still an amateur and signed professional forms for the club in March 1964. But it would be another four seasons before he made the goalkeeper's jersey his own. Wilson went on to play more than 350 games for the Gunners, winning league, FA Cup and European Fairs Cup honours. Despite being born in England, Wilson – on the basis of Scottish parentage – opted to play for Scotland and was capped twice in 1971. During the Double season Wilson was at his best, making two magnificent saves in the FA Cup final against Liverpool to keep Arsenal's Double dream alive. He was a brave goalkeeper, not unlike Bert Trautman in many ways; strong, committed and never afraid to hurl himself at the feet of marauding forwards. Wilson remained a regular in the side until a serious injury in the 1972 FA Cup semi-final saw him hobbling off the field. It was an injury that was to rule him out of the final. He remained at Highbury until 1974, when he surprised everyone by quitting to become a BBC Television sports presenter.

WIN – HIGHEST. Arsenal's highest victory in any official match was the 12–0 defeat of Loughborough in a division two fixture in March 1900. In December 1904, however, they defeated a Parisian XI 26–1 at Plumstead, but that has to be considered as an unofficial match.

WINS IN A SEASON – FEWEST. Arsenal's poorest league performance was in 1912–13, when they won only three matches out of their 38 league games and finished bottom of the first division with just 18 points.

WINS IN A SEASON – HIGHEST. In the 1970–71 season Arsenal won 29 of their 42 league fixtures to win the league title, the highest number of victories in the club's history.

WINTERBURN, NIGEL. After being released by Birmingham City, Winterburn spent four seasons with Wimbledon, where he eventually began to develop his potential. He won England under-21 honours as well as a regular place in the Wimbledon side, and in May 1987 he was signed by George Graham for £400,000. But even that kind of price did not guarantee a first-team place at Highbury. Indeed, it was not until 1988, with Kenny Sansom injured, that Winterburn made the breakthrough. But since getting into the side he has remained a permanent fixture, even though he missed a vital penalty in the League Cup final against Luton Town, a penalty that would have put the Gunners 3–1 ahead with only eight minutes remaining. As it was, Luton came back from the dead to win 3–2. Winterburn has now won two league championship medals, a League Cup winners medal, an FA Cup winners medal and then topped that with a European Cup Winners Cup medal in 1994 to prove that he is one of the shrewdest buys George Graham has yet made. He won his first England cap when he came on as a substitute against Italy in 1990.

WOOD, GEORGE. Goalkeeper signed from Everton for £150,000 in August 1980 as cover for Pat Jennings. It meant that Wood got few chances but when he did get an opportunity he grabbed it and even kept the great Irishman out of the side for the best part of a season after Jennings had been injured. But he was never popular with the Highbury crowd, especially when they compared him to Jennings. Wood, born in Scotland, won four Scottish caps between 1979 and 1982, with just one of these coming while he was at Highbury. In May 1983 he joined Crystal Palace on a free transfer.

WOODCOCK, TONY. Hugely expensive striker signed from Cologne for £500,000 during the 1982 close season. Woodcock had begun his playing days with Nottingham

Forest, joining them as an apprentice in 1972. He made his league debut in 1974 but showed little promise and, with so few opportunities at a City Ground bustling with talented strikers, he was allowed out on loan to Lincoln City and Doncaster Rovers. He eventually returned to Forest, was given his chance and was soon helping them towards the league championship, the European Cup and the League Cup, besides, picking up England honours as well. Woodcock was hot property and in November 1979 Forest sold him to Cologne for £650,000. He continued to sparkle in German football, showing great maturity and commitment, but decided on a return to English football where he felt he could win more honours. Arsenal jumped at the opportunity to sign him and in August 1982 he was leading the Gunners attack. Over the next four seasons he went on to play almost 200 games for the club, scoring 74 goals. He was the club's leading goalscorer in each of his four seasons, though there was always the feeling that perhaps he might have done better. His finest moment in an Arsenal shirt was undoubtedly his five goals at Villa Park as Arsenal beat Villa 6–2. His Highbury career, however, was solid rather than inspirational and he never quite showed the touches that made him such an exciting prospect under Brian Clough. It was pretty much the same with England. He won his first cap in 1979, collecting six caps with Forest. He picked up a further 33 caps with Cologne but only three while at Highbury. He scored 16 goals for England, a useful scoring rate but it never really brought much in the way of luck or honours for his country. Injuries eventually began to affect his Arsenal career and in 1986–87, unable to agree new terms, he returned to Cologne for £140,000.

WOOLWICH ARSENAL. The name of the club between 1891 and 1914.

WORLD CUP. Many Arsenal players have appeared in World Cup games and in the World Cup finals but, surprisingly, no Arsenal player appeared in the 1966 England World Cup winning side. There was only one Arsenal man

Billy Wright

in the England squad and that was George Eastham, who in fact did not get a game during the finals. Alan Ball, however, who did play against West Germany in the final, later joined Arsenal.

WRIGHT, BILLY. One of the great names of British football whose four-year spell as Arsenal manager promised much but in the end delivered little. The golden-haired former Wolves and England captain was named as Arsenal manager in May 1962. Wright had not long retired from the game after winning 105 England caps and had just held the position as coach of the England youth and under–23 sides. His appointment was something of a surprise and also a gamble, given that Wright had never held any managerial posts. But it was a popular choice. He began well with the signing of Joe Baker, the Torino striker. In his first season Arsenal finished in a respectable seventh spot but had conceded 79 goals. As a result, Wright plunged into the transfer market, signing the Dundee centre-half Ian Ure. But it did little good. The following season they finished eighth and had conceded 82 goals. Further defensive reinforcements

Ian Wright

were called in, with Frank McLintock and Don Howe joining the club, while goalkeeper Bob Wilson was given his first chance, but the difference was only marginal as Arsenal slipped further down the table. Arsenal were also knocked out of the FA Cup by Peterborough and in May 1966 a mere 4,554 turned up at Highbury to see Leeds United win 3–0. The fans had spoken and that summer Wright was duly sacked. It had all been too much for the former England captain. A genial, quiet man, Wright probably lacked the toughness to be a successful manager. He made some intelligent signings but the club was at one of its lowest points since the war and it needed an inspirational manager to pull it out of the doldrums. Sadly, Wright was not the man. After Highbury he decided that football management was not for him and he joined Associated Television in the Midlands as a sports executive.

WRIGHT, IAN. One of the great goalscorers of the modern game, Wright joined Crystal Palace during the 1985 close season and made his debut shortly afterwards against Huddersfield Town. At first the goals came slowly but after a couple of seasons at Palace he hit 20 league goals in the 1987–88 campaign. The following season he went even better, knocking in 24 as Crystal Palace won promotion to the first division. A couple of broken legs in his first season in division one kept his goalscoring down but he did manage to play in the FA Cup final against Manchester United, coming on as a substitute to score two spectacular goals. In the replay he was surprisingly left on the bench, only reappearing when it was too late. The following season, 1990–91, back to full fitness, he hit 20 league goals and won his first England cap, against Cameroon. Then early in the 1991–92 season Arsenal stepped in with a surprise £2.5 million record-breaking bid that brought him to Highbury. In his first game he was on the mark and then hit a hat trick on his league debut for the Gunners. At the end of that season he topped the Gunners goalscoring charts with 24 League goals. In all, he had scored 29 goals that season to make him the division's top scorer. The following season, 1992–93, he was even more devastating, with 15 league goals, 10 in the FA Cup and five in the Coca-Cola Cup, to earn him a League Cup winners medal and an FA Cup winners medal. In the FA Cup final he scored Arsenal's only goal against Sheffield Wednesday and then hit another goal in the replay. During the 1993–94 season he hit 34 goals, 23 of them in the league, but missed out on the European Cup Winners Cup final because of suspension. With Alan Shearer the regular choice for England, Wright's international appearances have been limited but he still has well over a dozen caps to his name and looks set to win many more. Wright is a quick-thinking, lively striker with exceptional pace and is now one of the most popular players at Highbury and has become something of a media personality as well.

X. In football X traditionally stands for draw. The club record for the number of draws in a season was in 1969–70 when they drew 18 out of 42 matches.

XMAS DAY. There was a time when football was regularly played on Christmas Day but in recent years the footballing authorities have dropped the fixture from their calendar. The last time Arsenal played on a Christmas Day was in 1957, when they drew 1–1 at Chelsea in a first division match. One of the most memorable Christmas Day games was in 1952 when Arsenal beat Bolton Wanderers 6–4 at Burnden Park before a crowd of over 47,000. Interestingly, when Arsenal moved to Highbury in 1913 they leased the land from St John's College of Divinity and included in the 12-year lease agreement was a stipulation that they would not play football at the ground on either Good Friday or Christmas Day. It was not until 1934, when the lease had come to an end, that any games were played on those particular days at Highbury.

Y

YEAR. Arsenal Football Club was formed in October 1886 at the Prince of Wales public house in Plumstead. It was originally called Dial Square FC but in December of that same year it was decided to change the club's name to Royal Arsenal.

YOUNG PLAYER OF THE YEAR. The annual award of Young Player of the Year has gone to two Arsenal players:
1987 Tony Adams
1989 Paul Merson.

YOUNG, WILLIE. Tall, lanky central defender who came to Arsenal in 1977 for £80,000. It was the second time Terry Neill had signed him, having brought him down from Aberdeen to Tottenham 18 months earlier. At Highbury Neill needed someone to slot in alongside David O'Leary in defence and Young looked the ideal candidate. It was not altogether successful. Young was slow at times and his distribution left much to be desired, but he had plenty of commitment and his sheer size and look was enough to terrify defenders. His 6 feet 3 inches height also gave the Gunners some additional aerial power at both ends of the pitch. He scored 20 goals in his Highbury career, many of them with his head, and played more than 250 games. He won an FA Cup winners medal in 1979 but after a disagreement with Terry Neill he joined Nottingham Forest for £170,000 in December 1981. He later played with Norwich and Brighton but had clearly seen his best days at Highbury. He was a Scottish under–23 international but was never capped at full level by his country.

YOUNGEST PLAYER. The youngest player ever to pull on an Arsenal shirt is Gerry Ward, who was just 16 years old when he played for Arsenal against Huddersfield Town in August 1953.

YOUTH CUP. Arsenal first participated in the FA Youth Cup in 1954. They have reached the final on four occasions, winning the competition three times:
1965 Everton 3 Arsenal 2 (aggregate)
1966 Arsenal 5 Sunderland 3 (aggregate)
1971 Arsenal 2 Cardiff 0 (aggregate)
1988 Arsenal 6 Doncaster Rovers 1 (aggregate)

Z

ZENITH. Arsenal fans could argue long into the night about when the club reached its zenith. During the 1930s they won four league titles and appeared in three FA Cup finals, winning the Cup twice. In the immediate post-war years Arsenal won the title in 1947–48, then again in 1952–53, won the Cup in 1950 and were losers in 1952. Then, of course, there is 1970–71, when Arsenal became only the second club this century to achieve the Double, adding the two trophies to the European Fairs Cup they had won the year before. Others might say that the current Arsenal side is the best ever, having won two league titles, the FA Cup, the League Cup and the European Cup Winners Cup under George Graham's management.